GILL MACLENNAN'S
CHOCOLATE

GILL MACLENNAN'S
CHOCOLATE

MEREHURST

A big thank-you goes to my Mum who came down to help me do a final test on my shortlist of recipes, even though she had just started the Hay diet.
Every recipe in this book has been eaten by a selection of eager tasters and their success judged by the speed at which they disappeared from the plate. Thanks go to all the staff and teachers at Hampton Infant School who wrote very clear top-of-the-class reports, all my colleagues at work who cheerfully tucked in at 9.30am and everyone at Martin's work who sent e mail messages asking for the recipes.
A huge thank-you to Roger, Michelle, Jacqueline and Rebecca for making the pictures so stunning and to Maureen for making sure the recipes made sense.

First published in 1996 by Merehurst Limited,
Ferry House, 51-57 Lacy Road, Putney, London SW15 1PR

Copyright © Merehurst Limited 1996

ISBN 1-85391-561-0

A catalogue record for this book is available from the British Library.

The right of Gill MacLennan to be identified as the Author of this work has been asserted by her in accordance with the Copyright, Designs and Patents Act 1988.

Editor: Maureen Callis
Designer: Roger Hammond
Photographer: Michelle Garrett
Home economist: Jacqueline Clark
Home economist's assistant: Emma Gow
Stylist: Rebecca Gillies
Typesetter: Mike Weintroub
Front cover photographs by Sue Baker

Colour separation by Fotographics Ltd UK, Hong Kong
Printed in Singapore by CS Graphics Pte Ltd

Frontispiece: Chocolate and Vanilla Fence filled with The Ultimate Chocolate Mousse, recipes on pages 28 and 29.

FOREWORD

There can be few foods that arouse such passions as chocolate. I love cooking, I enjoy eating and I adore chocolate. I have been collecting recipes since I was about nine and knew from a very early age that I wanted to cook. In the early days it was the childhood favourites like chocolate Krispies, sticky with golden syrup, and good old Victoria Sandwich cake, meticulously creamed with a wooden spoon in a big beige china mixing bowl. I would carefully write the recipes into my own book with a fountain pen and my best writing. Through school and college I would tear recipes out of magazines and stick them in a big scrapbook which I would read and re-read the way other children read comics.

I have been a cookery writer now for over 15 years, author of two other cookery books and had the good fortune to work in the cookery departments of top womens' magazines like Family Circle and Woman's Realm and be cookery editor of Woman. One of the most wonderful things about working on magazines was the readers, who would phone up or write to us asking for a recipe they had tried, liked but lost. You could guarantee that chocolate recipes would be the most requested.

This is the cream of my collection – gathered from top chefs, inspired by puddings I've eaten in restaurants, developed in magazine test kitchens, passed on by friends and invented in my own kitchen. There's a mix of classics that cannot be improved upon and some new creations of my own (like the easiest and I think most delicious ice cream ever). Chocolate goes well with so many different flavours, including the warm spices like cinnamon and nutmeg; the great family of nuts; the orchard fruits like pears, plums and cherries; and all the soft summer berries like redcurrants and strawberries. I like it with vanilla; with the tangy citrus flavours of oranges and lemons; and with coffee.

In here you will find everything from a throw-it-all-in-the-bowl-and-beat-it chocolate cake that's ideal for children's parties to the most wonderful cakes special enough for Christmas, weddings and anniversaries. There is a drop-dead hot chocolate soufflé with a whole Chocolate Orange baked in the middle of it, the best coffee puddle pudding, the stickiest brownies, the most wonderful chunky chocolate cookies and the creamiest New York style cheesecake made with white chocolate. I want you to try the fudgiest no-cook chocolate cake (a recipe prized out of my Mum), the chocolate bread and the blueberry pudding which is like nothing else I have ever eaten. And then of course there are the muffins, tart with raspberries and laden with chunks of Swiss white chocolate . . .

A passion for chocolate? You bet!

Gill MacLennan

Introduction

Hot puddings

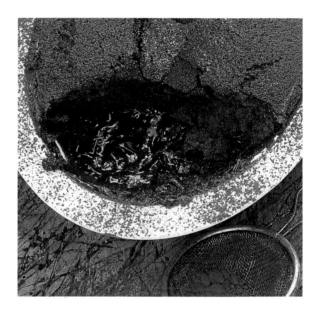

Cold puddings

Biscuits and cookies

page 50

Everyday cakes

page 66

Special cakes and bakes

page 82

INTRODUCTION

Although there seem to be lots of self-confessed chocoholics around, who eat chocolate daily, I think of it as something that I eat from time to time and savour. Because of this I recommend using the best quality chocolate you can buy. The higher the cocoa solids, the better the quality – cost is not always a true indication of that. I have tested all these recipes using a top quality, supermarket brand cooking chocolate with a great taste at a good price. In recent years chocolate has been taken as seriously as wine, with experts recommending chocolate made from a particular bean or grown from a single estate. Like fine wines, these bars are expensive and best reserved for eating, not slinging into a chocolate cake – you wouldn't glug a special and expensive bottle of wine into a casserole!

To get the best results, choose a chocolate that has a stated amount of cocoa solids in it. This will be printed on the label. On the whole I have used 50% cocoa solids but occasionally 75%. Each recipe lists the recommended level. Even if you are not a dark chocolate lover, you need to start off with something intensely chocolatey when cooking, because the flavour gets diluted once you mix it with other ingredients. I used to be a Galaxy® girl but I am coming round to the darker chocolates. My own weakness is for white chocolate which is not really chocolate but adds a special something to so many dishes. It works brilliantly with tart fruits like blueberries, lemons and raspberries, as well as coconut and vanilla.

Whatever you do, I don't recommend chocolate flavour cake covering. Better to make a splendid chocolate pudding occasionally with the real thing than something with a poor flavour more often.

MELTING CHOCOLATE

Chocolate melts best if it is broken into small, even-sized pieces and is melted slowly. There are three main methods:

In the microwave

I find that if you use a glass bowl, the chocolate can scorch so I always use a large plastic measuring jug or plastic plate. Stir half-way through the recommended time. I use this method with great success.

In a non-stick pan

This works well, especially on gas where you can control the heat. Keep the heat low and keep an eye on it all the time. Stir, especially round the edge, until the chocolate has melted but is not hot.

Over hot water

This is my least favourite because it seems to be a bit fiddly but it is probably the most gentle and the most used. Bring a small pan of water to simmering and place a bowl over the top, making sure that the bottom of the bowl is clear of the water. Add the chocolate and allow to melt, stirring occasionally.

PLEASE READ THIS BEFORE YOU START
COOKING

A standard spoon measurement is used in all the recipes

5 ml spoon = 1 teaspoon

10 ml spoon = 2 teaspoon

15 ml spoon = 1 tablespoon

All spoon measures are level

• Ovens should be preheated to the specified temperature. All the recipes were tested in a conventional oven and baked on the centre shelf. If you have a fan-assisted oven, check the manufacturer's handbook to adjust the cooking times. It will cook hotter and faster so you will have to lower the temperature and reduce the cooking time.

• My microwave is 800 watt power and has a turntable. Check the wattage on your oven and add or take away time if it is less or more powerful. As a rule of thumb, cook for an extra 10 seconds a minute for every 50 watts power less than 800 watts.

• I tested all the recipes in metric because, now that manufacturers are packing ingredients in metric, I found it more practical. However, for all recipes, quantities are given in metric and imperial. Follow one set of measurements but not a mixture as they are not interchangeable.

• Where practical, I used a full pack of ingredients and have listed it following the manufacturer's metric pack size – for example

butter, which comes in 250 g blocks. For a recipe which relies on a proportion of ingredients to work – say a cake – you may find that 250 g butter to 125 g sugar is given as 8 oz to 4 oz. On other recipes 200 g to 100 g may also be listed as 8 oz to 4 oz. Do not worry about these inconsistencies – the recipes have been worked out so that the proportions work and you use a whole pack of something if possible.

• As I write, there are plans that small 142 ml (5 fl oz) and 284 ml (10 fl oz) cartons of cream are to be re-sized to 150 ml and 300 ml for a small or a large tub respectively. The difference between 142 ml and 150 ml is 1½ teaspoons and won't make any noticeable difference to the success of a recipe.

• British Government recommendations are that no-one should eat raw eggs, particularly the elderly, young children, the sick and pregnant women, because of the risk of salmonella infection. I have included some recipes in this book which do use raw eggs because I think they are too good to leave out. If you decide to make them I recommend that you buy free-range eggs from a salmonella-tested flock.

• I have used butter in most of the recipes because it has a great flavour and is natural. If you use margarine instead, use a good quality, full-fat variety – the low-fat types contain too much water and will not give the same results.

Hot puddings

There's a great mix in here of favourite family puddings and dinner party desserts. From the most comforting nursery puddings like crumble, steamed sponge and a self-saucing chocolate pudding to splendid but simple special desserts like soufflés, this chapter shows that a hot pudding doesn't have to be a heavy pudding.

CHOCOLATE CHRISTMAS PUDDING

Time to make: 40 minutes
Time to cook: 3 to 6 hours

Makes 3 x 900 g (2 lb) puddings

300 g (10 oz) carrot

1 orange

1 lemon

200 g (8 oz) soft light brown sugar

200 g (8 oz) raisins

200 g (8 oz) sultanas

200 g (8 oz) currants

200 g (8 oz) suet

100 g (4 oz) fresh white breadcrumbs

100 g (4 oz) white chocolate drops

100 g (4 oz) dark chocolate drops

100 g (4 oz) milk chocolate drops

100 g (4 oz) plain flour

25 g (1 oz) cocoa powder

¼ teaspoon allspice

¼ teaspoon grated nutmeg

¼ teaspoon ground cinnamon

¼ teaspoon ground cloves

¼ teaspoon ground black pepper

½ teaspoon ground ginger

100 ml (4 fl oz) milk

If you think of Christmas pudding as being dense and heavy, then you are in for a very pleasant surprise. This recipe is based on my Granny Rootfield's traditional pudding which is lightened with carrots and has very little flour in it. The chocolate adds an amazing velvety texture. Serve with a scoop of good vanilla ice cream, or thin vanilla custard.

1   Look out three 900 g (2 lb) pudding basins and grease well. Coarsely grate the carrot. Finely grate the rind from the orange and lemon and squeeze the juices. Put the carrot, orange and lemon rind and juices in a very large mixing bowl.

2   Add the sugar, raisins, sultanas, currants, suet, breadcrumbs and all the chocolate drops.

3   Put a sieve over the bowl and add the flour, cocoa powder, allspice, nutmeg, cinnamon, cloves, pepper and ginger. Sift in and stir to mix.

4   Finally add the milk and stir very thoroughly until everything is evenly combined. (At this point, everyone in our family closes their eyes, stirs the pudding mixture and makes a secret wish.)

5   Divide the mixture between the prepared pudding basins, cover with greaseproof paper and then foil. Secure with string and tie a handle to get the puddings in and out of the saucepan easily.

6   Put each pudding in a deep, lidded saucepan. Fill with boiling water to come halfway up the side of the basin. Return the water to the boil then reduce to a simmer. Cover and steam for 3 to 6 hours, topping up from time to time with boiling water. (The longer you steam it the better it is.)

7   Remove the foil and greaseproof paper and spoon out of the basin to serve, or run a palette knife around the pudding to loosen it from the basin and invert onto a serving plate. Serve at once.

Cook's Tips
Choose a pudding basin with a rim so that you can easily secure the foil and greaseproof with string.
Once cooked the puddings can be cooled and stored in a cool, dark place or in a freezer for up to one year. To serve: repeat step 6, cooking for 1 to 2 hours to heat through.

HOT CHOCOLATE SOUFFLÉ

Time to make: 25 minutes
Time to bake: 25 to 30 minutes

Serves 4 to 6

25 g (1 oz) caster sugar
150 g (6 oz) dark chocolate, 70% cocoa solids
250 ml (10 fl oz) milk
50 g (2 oz) soft light brown sugar
25 g (1 oz) butter
25 g (1 oz) plain flour
4 medium eggs, size 3
1 tablespoon icing sugar

If you can make a basic white sauce, you can make a superb chocolate soufflé. There is nothing difficult about it. This is my basic recipe. I vary it depending on my guests, adding chopped After Eight® mints or a spoonful or two of dark rum to the mixture or a scattering of roasted hazelnuts on top before baking. Serve with single cream. To turn great into outstanding, drop a whole Chocolate Orange into the middle of the dish, cover with the mixture and bake. You get this light, baked soufflé on the outside and a thick pool of melted orange chocolate in the middle. Simply amazing . . .

1 Look out a deep soufflé dish that measures 18 cm (7 in) across the top and is about 10 cm (4 in) high. Butter it and sprinkle with the caster sugar. Set the oven to 170C, 340F, Gas 3.
2 Break the chocolate into squares and put in a small non-stick pan. Add the milk and brown sugar and heat gently until the chocolate has melted. Remove from the heat.
3 Melt the butter in a large non-stick pan. Add the flour and stir for 1 minute to make a roux. Take the pan off the heat and gradually stir in the melted chocolate mixture. Return to the heat and boil, stirring, for 20 seconds. Remove from the heat and leave to cool a little.
4 Separate the eggs: put the yolks in a small cup and the whites in a large, clean, grease-free bowl. Whisk the egg whites until they are stiff but not too dry. Stir the egg yolks into the chocolate custard mixture, then lightly fold in the egg whites, using a metal spoon. Do not stir or beat the mixture.
5 Pour the mixture into the prepared soufflé dish. Bake for 25 to 30 minutes or until well risen and the outside feels firm around the edge. Quickly sift the icing sugar over the top and serve at once.

Cook's Tip
Make sure the egg whites are not overwhisked or they go dry and bob about the chocolate mixture, making them difficult to fold in.

HOT AND COLD SOUFFLÉS

Time to make: 15 minutes
Time to bake: 10 minutes

Makes 2

50 g (2 oz) dark chocolate, 70% cocoa solids

50 g (2 oz) butter

4 medium eggs, size 3

15 g (½ oz) caster sugar

15 g (½ oz) plain flour

2 tablespoons good vanilla ice cream (not soft scoop)

My thanks go to Jonathon for this amazing recipe. The soufflé changes character depending on the ice cream you use – try anything from a tart blackcurrant sorbet to the richest vanilla.

1 Look out two ramekins that measure 10 cm (4 in) across the top and grease well. Set the oven to 190C, 375F, Gas 5.
2 Break the chocolate into squares and put in a non-stick pan. Add the butter and heat gently until melted. Remove from heat.
3 Separate the eggs: put the yolks in a small mixing bowl and the whites in a large, clean, grease-free bowl. Add the sugar to the yolks and whisk until pale and creamy. Put a sieve over the bowl, add the flour, sift then fold in with the melted chocolate.
4 Whisk the egg whites until they are stiff but not too dry. Lightly fold into the chocolate mixture using a metal spoon.
5 Pour into the ramekins to half-fill them. Put a small scoop of ice cream in the middle and cover with the remaining mixture.
6 Bake at once for 10 minutes or until well risen and firm around the edge. Serve at once.

QUICK WHITE SOUFFLÉS

Time to make: 15 minutes
Time to bake: 10 to 12 minutes

Makes 2

100 g (4 oz) good quality white chocolate

4 tablespoons double cream

2 medium eggs, size 3

These soufflés are quick and easy. Serve with a tart sauce like fresh raspberries puréed with a little icing sugar then sieved, or a fresh mango puréed with a little lemon or lime juice.

1 Look out two deep ramekins that measure 10 cm (4 in) across the top and grease well. Set the oven to 200C, 400F, Gas 6.
2 Break the chocolate into squares, put in a small non-stick pan with the cream and heat gently until the chocolate has melted.
3 Separate the eggs: put the yolks in a cup and the whites in a clean, grease-free bowl. Whisk the whites until stiff but not too dry. Stir the yolks into the chocolate, then lightly fold in the whites.
4 Pour into the ramekins. Bake for 10 to 12 minutes or until well risen and firm around the edge. Serve at once.

WHITE CHOCOLATE & LEMON BREAD AND BUTTER PUDDING

Time to make: 20 minutes plus
   15 minutes standing time
Time to bake: 20 minutes

Serves 4

5 slices fresh white bread

25 g (1 oz) unsalted butter, at room temperature

4 tablespoons good quality lemon curd

150 g (6 oz) good quality white chocolate

150 ml (5 fl oz) milk

150 ml (5 fl oz) double cream

2 egg yolks

25 g (1 oz) sultanas

This is a lovely pudding, light and lemony yet creamy and rich in vanilla. Make it with fresh bread and choose a top quality lemon curd. Good apricot jam makes a delicious substitute.

1 Look out a 1.4 litre (2 pt) oval ovenproof dish and butter lightly.
2 Cut the crusts off the bread and give to the birds. Spread the bread thinly with butter and half of the lemon curd. Cut into triangles.
3 Break the chocolate into pieces and put in a small non-stick pan. Add the milk and cream and heat gently until the chocolate has melted. Bring to the boil then remove from the heat.
4 Whisk the egg yolks in a large mixing bowl and pour the melted chocolate mixture onto them. Whisk constantly to make a custard.
5 Arrange half of the bread in the bottom of the prepared dish, sprinkle with the sultanas and pour over enough custard to moisten.
6 Cover with the remaining bread, arranging it neatly, and pour over the rest of the custard. Leave to stand for 15 minutes. Set the oven to 180C, 350F, Gas 4.
7 Bake the pudding for 20 minutes until just set and the top is golden. Brush with the remaining lemon curd and serve hot with whipped cream.

Cook's Tips
Make sure the butter is soft and spreadable.
Choose a lemon curd that is as close to homemade as you can get – it should have lemons, butter and eggs in it. Avoid any with gelling agents, thickeners, artificial flavourings and colourings.

RHUBARB WITH WHITE CHOCOLATE CRUMBLE

Time to make: 15 minutes
Time to bake: 30 minutes

Serves 2 to 3

350 g (12 oz) fresh, young, pink rhubarb

100 g (4 oz) good quality white chocolate

100 g (4 oz) plain flour

50 g (2 oz) unsalted butter

25 g (1 oz) caster sugar

This is a simple but delicious family pudding which I serve with thin pouring cream or a fresh orange sauce. It's good enough to serve at a dinner party, too: make four individual puddings and serve topped with good vanilla ice cream, a small scoop of orange sorbet or a spoonful of clotted cream.

1 Look out a 1.4 litre (2 pt) ovenproof oval baking dish. Set the oven to 180C, 350F, Gas 4.
2 Trim the rhubarb and cut into short lengths. Pile into the baking dish and shake level.
3 To make the crumble: break the chocolate into pieces. Put in a food processor bowl with the flour and process until the mixture resembles breadcrumbs.
4 Add the butter and sugar and process again until the mixture begins to stick together. Remove the blade from the bowl and squeeze the mixture between your hands to gather the coarse crumbs into loose clusters. Scatter over the rhubarb.
5 Cover with foil and bake for 15 minutes. Remove the foil and bake for a further 15 minutes or until the rhubarb is soft and bubbling and the crumble is golden.

Cook's Tips
Each brand of white chocolate seems to melt differently. I use a good quality Swiss chocolate bar (not the sort you would normally give to children) or an own-label Deluxe White Chocolate specially for cooking from my local supermarket. Avoid white chocolate flavour cake covering which is much poorer quality and will not give a good flavour.
This crumble topping is also good over other tart fruits like gooseberries, brambles (blackberries) or plums.

MICROWAVED CHOCOLATE PUDDING

Time to make: 15 minutes

Time to bake: 3 minutes in a microwave, 1 to 2 hours steamed

Serves 4

2 medium eggs, size 3

100 g (4 oz) dark chocolate, 50% cocoa solids

1 tablespoon milk

100 g (4 oz) butter, at room temperature

100 g (4 oz) soft light brown sugar

50 g (2 oz) fresh white breadcrumbs

75 g (3 oz) self-raising flour

One of the greatest joys of owning a microwave is that you can be sitting down to a comforting plate of 'steamed' pudding in about 20 minutes from first thinking about it. This recipe makes a wonderful light pudding. Serve with a Hot Chocolate Sauce, see page 25, a fresh orange sauce or even a brandy- or rum-flavoured butter.

1   Look out a 1.4 litre (2 pt) microwave-proof pudding basin. Crack the eggs into a mug and beat lightly.

2   Break the chocolate into squares and put in a bowl with the milk. Melt in the microwave or over a pan of hot water.

3   Put the butter and sugar in a mixing bowl and beat until light and creamy. Add the eggs a little a time, beating well between each addition.

4   Whisk in the melted chocolate, then fold in the breadcrumbs.

5   Put a sieve over the bowl, add the flour, sift then fold in with a metal spoon. Spoon into the pudding basin.

6   Cover the top with non-pvc clear film. Peel back the film on two sides to leave a 1 cm (½ in) gap.

7   Microwave for 3 minutes on Full Power (100%). Leave to stand for 5 minutes.

8   Serve from the basin or run a palette knife around the edge to loosen the pudding and turn out onto a serving plate. Eat at once.

TO STEAM THE PUDDING

Follow the recipe up to the end of step 5.

6   Look out a double sheet of greaseproof paper and cut it into a circle 10 cm (4 in) larger than the top of a 1.4 litre (2 pt) pudding basin. Place on top and cover with foil. Secure with string, leaving enough for a handle to get the pudding in and out of a saucepan.

7   Put the pudding in a deep, lidded saucepan. Fill with boiling water to come halfway up the side of the basin. Bring back to the boil, then reduce to a simmer. Cover and steam for at least 1 hour or up to 2 hours, topping up from time to time with boiling water.

8   Take the pudding out of the pan and remove the foil and greaseproof. Serve as above.

CHOCOLATE PUDDLE PUDDING

Time to make: 20 minutes
Time to bake: 40 minutes

Serves 4 to 6

2 medium eggs, size 3

75 g (3 oz) dark chocolate, 50% cocoa solids

2 teaspoons instant coffee granules

1 tablespoon cocoa powder

3 tablespoons boiling water

100 g (4 oz) butter, at room temperature

100 g (4 oz) soft light brown sugar

100 g (4 oz) self-raising flour

Sauce

25 g (1 oz) cocoa powder

1 tablespoon boiling water

300 ml (10 fl oz) milk

100 g (4 oz) soft light brown sugar

This is a glorious pudding. It is such an odd and improbable recipe that I wonder how it was ever invented. But it does work. It goes into the oven as a cake mixture on the bottom with some sweetened, cocoa-flavoured milk poured on top of it. When it is ready, you have a light sponge on the top and a thick, smooth chocolate custard on the bottom.

1   Look out a 1.4 litre (2 pt) oval ovenproof baking dish and grease well. Set the oven to 150C, 300F, Gas 1.
2   Crack the eggs into a mug and beat lightly. Chop the chocolate into rough chunks.
3   Spoon the coffee granules, cocoa powder and water into a mug and stir well to mix.
4   Put the butter and sugar in a mixing bowl and beat until light and creamy. Beat in the eggs, a little at a time, to make a light, fluffy mixture.
5   Beat in the cocoa mixture. Put a sieve over the bowl, add the flour, sift then fold in with a metal spoon. Fold in the chocolate. Spoon the mixture into the prepared dish and level the top.
6   To make the sauce: spoon the cocoa powder into a measuring jug and add the water. Stir well to dissolve the cocoa powder. Add the milk and sugar and whisk well to mix. Pour over the pudding mixture.
7   Bake for 40 minutes or until the centre is just set. Leave to stand for 5 minutes. Serve hot.

Cook's Tip
If the pudding is still a bit soft in the middle, the sauce will be thin when you cut into the pudding. However, if you overcook the pudding so that it is very firm in the centre and shrinking from the side of the dish, the sauce will disappear. The centre should spring back when you press it lightly with your fingertips.

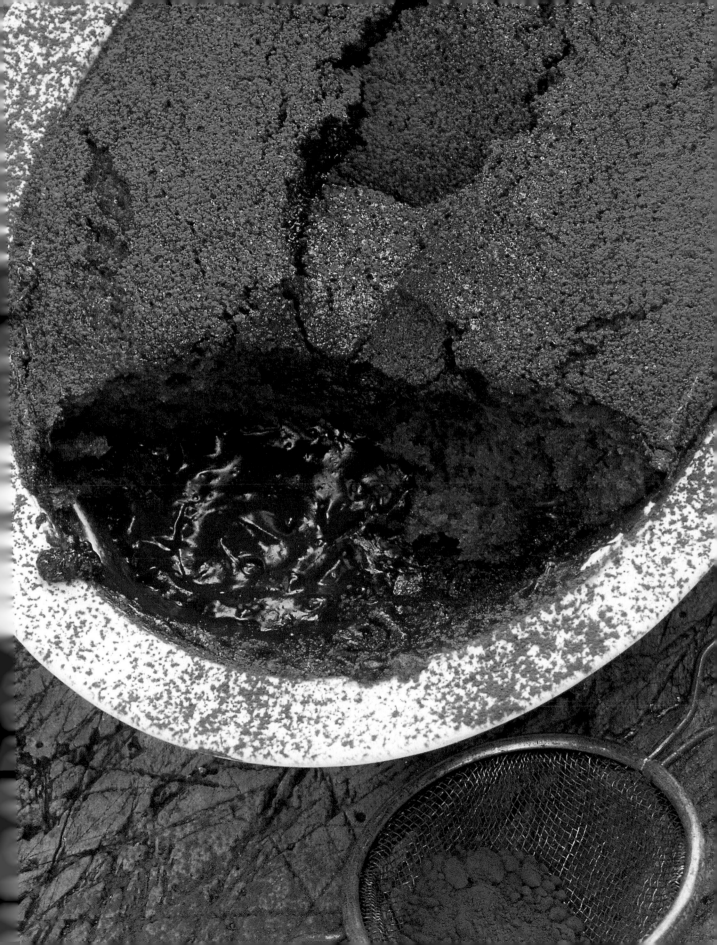

GREEK HONEY AND HAZELNUT PUDDINGS

Time to make: 15 minutes
Time to bake: 25 minutes

Makes 4

50 g (2 oz) roasted, chopped hazelnuts

2 tablespoons cocoa powder

½ teaspoon baking powder

100 g (4 oz) self-raising flour

100 ml (4 fl oz) milk

100 ml (4 fl oz) olive oil

2 tablespoons Greek mountain honey (or other well-flavoured clear honey)

1 medium egg, size 3

75 g (3 oz) soft light brown sugar

Serve with Greek-style yogurt or Hot Chocolate Sauce, see recipe on page 25

1   Look out four 300 ml (½ pt) metal pudding basins. Brush with oil and sprinkle with flour. Stand the basins in a baking tin to keep them together. Set the oven to 170C, 340F, Gas 3.
2   Put the hazelnuts in a food processor and process until they make a fine paste.
3   Put a sieve over the food processor bowl and add the cocoa powder, baking powder and flour. Sift in, then pulse the machine to mix well.
4   Pour the milk and oil into a large measuring jug. Add the honey, egg and sugar and beat lightly to mix.
5   Add the milk mixture to the hazelnut mixture and process to make a smooth batter. Run a spatula around the bowl to loosen any hazelnut paste, then give the machine one final burst.
6   Pour the mixture into the prepared basins and bake for 25 minutes or until the puddings are well risen and a knife inserted into the centre comes out clean. Leave to cool for 5 minutes.
7   Cut off the tops with a serrated knife and loosen the sides with a small palette knife. Turn out the puddings onto individual serving plates.

Cook's Tip
For a really professional presentation, I've taken a tip from top chef Tessa Bramley. Turn out each pudding onto a large serving plate. Pour thin hot custard round the pudding and thin Hot Chocolate Sauce round the custard. Where the custard and chocolate sauce meet, make circular patterns all the way round the pudding to swirl the two sauces together. Serve at once.

BAKED CHOCOLATE MOUSSE

Time to make: 15 minutes
Time to bake: 10 to 12 minutes

Makes 6

100 g (4 oz) dark chocolate, 75% cocoa solids
100 g (4 oz) unsalted butter
2 medium eggs, size 3, plus 2 yolks
150 g (6 oz) caster sugar
50 g (2 oz) self-raising flour

This is a truly wonderful pudding – very light, with an intensely chocolate flavour and a runny chocolate sauce in the middle. It is very quick to mix together and bakes in under 15 minutes so I rely on it a lot for through-the-week food for friends. Serve with lots of double cream or a fruity purée of sieved raspberries or blackcurrants.

1 Look out six 7.5 x 3.5 cm (3 x 1½ in) ramekins and grease well. Place on a baking tray. Set the oven to 180C, 350F, Gas 4.
2 Break the chocolate into pieces, put in a non-stick pan with the butter and heat gently until melted. Remove from the heat.
3 Put the eggs, egg yolks and sugar in a large measuring jug and whisk with an electric whisk for 2 minutes until the mixture is pale and creamy.
4 Pour the melted chocolate into the egg mixture and whisk to mix.
5 Put a sieve over the measuring jug, add the flour and sift, then whisk in until just mixed.
6 Pour the mixture into the prepared ramekins and bake for 10 to 12 minutes or until the tops are just dry and the puddings have risen.
7 Run a sharp knife around the inside of the ramekin and invert each pudding onto a serving plate. Serve at once. (When you cut into the puddings, the centre should be soft and runny.)

Cook's Tips
Watch the baking time carefully – do not overcook.
Any puddings not needed hot can be served cold – the middle will still be soft. Top with a sweetened mascarpone dusted with cocoa powder and cinnamon.

WHITE CHOCOLATE AND BLUEBERRY PUDDING

Time to make: 20 minutes
Time to bake: 45 to 50 minutes

Serves 6

150 g (6 oz) good quality white chocolate

200 g (8 oz) self-raising flour

150 g (6 oz) unsalted butter

50 g (2 oz) ground almonds

75 g (3 oz) caster sugar

2 medium eggs, size 3

4 tablespoons milk

1 teaspoon natural vanilla essence

250 g (9 oz) fresh or frozen blueberries

This is a wonderful, comforting, very 90s pud – very light-textured almond sponge with chunks of white chocolate and pockets of blueberries. Serve with cream whipped with good lemon curd or a simple lemon sauce.

1 Look out a 1.4 litre (2 pt) oval ovenproof dish. Set the oven to 170C, 340F, Gas 3. Chop the chocolate into rough chunks.
2 Sift the flour into a food processor. Add the butter and process until the mixture looks like breadcrumbs. Add the almonds and sugar and pulse the machine again to mix them in.
3 Beat the eggs, milk and vanilla essence together in a mug. Add to the flour mixture and process to make a very thick batter.
4 Remove the central blade from the machine and lightly stir in the chocolate and blueberries.
5 Pour the mixture into the baking dish and bake for 45 to 50 minutes or until well risen and golden. Serve warm.

Cook's Tip
This mixture can also be cooked and served as a cake. Look out a 20 cm (8 in) round, deep, loose-bottomed cake tin. Line the base and side with greaseproof paper. Using a scraper, transfer the mixture to the prepared tin and level the top. Bake for 1 hour or until the centre feels firm and the cake has begun to shrink from the side of the tin. Cool in the tin. Turn out and peel off the lining paper when completely cold. Cut into wedges to serve.

FIVE-MINUTE FONDUE

Time to make: 5 minutes

Serves 4

1 large Toblerone® or other similar chocolate bar

5 tablespoons single cream

This was invented for my father-in-law who has a sweet tooth and eats chocolate every day. The fondue changes depending on the chocolate bar you use – most brands melt quite successfully. Serve with fresh fruit like strawberries, apricots, apple slices, bananas and cherries, using a cocktail stick to swirl them in the fondue. Allow 450 g (1 lb) prepared fresh fruit for 4 people.

1 Break the chocolate into pieces and put in a small non-stick pan. Add the cream and heat gently until the chocolate has melted. Remove from the heat and stir well.
2 Pour into a serving bowl and serve at once.

Cook's Tip
Avoid fruits like melon and fresh oranges for dipping. They are too wet and the chocolate slides off them.

MARS® BAR SAUCE

Time to make: 5 minutes

Serves 4

2 standard size Mars® bars

3 tablespoons single cream or milk

This is so simple but so good that I have to include it. It is a wonderful sauce to pour over ice cream but I have served it as a two-person fondue, too. It is also brilliant cooled and poured into the White Chocolate Ice Cream on page 37 to give a fudgy chocolate ripple.

1 Cut the Mars® bars into chunks and put in a small non-stick pan with the cream or milk.
2 Melt slowly over a low heat then bring to just below boiling. Remove from the heat.
3 Beat until smooth and shiny and use at once.

Cook's Tip
If you are the sort of person who keeps Mars® bars in the fridge, it's best to let them come to room temperature first.

HOT CHOCOLATE SAUCE

Time to make: 10 minutes

Makes 300 ml (10 fl oz)

150 g (6 oz) dark chocolate,
50% cocoa solids

150 ml (5 fl oz) double cream

25 g (1 oz) butter

25 g (1 oz) icing sugar

A great all-round sauce that's good on profiteroles, crêpes, ice cream and cakes.

1 Break the chocolate into pieces, put in a small non-stick pan with the cream and butter and heat gently until melted. Remove from the heat.
2 Beat in the icing sugar and keep beating until the sauce is smooth and glossy.
3 Reheat until just beginning to boil. Remove from the heat and beat well.

Cook's Tip
This sauce will keep well in the fridge for up to three days. Reheat gently before serving

CHOCOLATE GANACHE

Time to make: 10 minutes

250 g (9 oz) plain chocolate

200 ml (7 fl oz) double cream

I probably use this icing more than any other because it is straightforward and tastes brilliant. It is a classic with a pure chocolate flavour and smooth, silky texture. I use it over profiteroles, as a sauce for ice cream and to fill cakes.

1 Break the chocolate into pieces and put in a large heatproof bowl.
2 Pour the cream into a small pan and bring to the boil. Pour it over the chocolate, cover with a plate and leave for 5 minutes.
3 Using a balloon whisk, gradually whisk the mixture until it is smooth and glossy. Pour over a dessert or cake or leave to cool until it is thick enough to spread and fill a cake.

Cold puddings

The list here reads like the most tantalising dessert menu. Will you go for the to-die-for cheesecake, a slice of the buttery Pecan and Maple Pie, the Charlotte, the tower of chocolate meringues, the brûlée of white chocolate and ginger or the chocolate truffle cake with its amazing white chocolate scrolls? Or perhaps a little of each?

PLUM, ALMOND AND WHITE CHOCOLATE TART

Time to make: 25 minutes
Time to bake: 45 to 50 minutes

Serves 6 to 8

375 g (13 oz) packet sweet shortcrust pastry

6 ripe plums

2 medium eggs, size 3

300 g (10 oz) good quality white chocolate

25 g (1 oz) unblanched almonds

50 g (2 oz) unsalted butter, at room temperature

50 g (2 oz) soft light brown sugar

100 g (4 oz) ground almonds

There is a lot of white chocolate in here and it makes an unforgettable filling in this tart. It was inspired by a tart we bought at a Sunday market in France. If you can warm each slice through in the microwave just before serving, I think you get the flavour of the almonds and the texture of the chocolate at their best. This is also good as a pudding, straight from the oven, with whipped cream or a thin vanilla custard.

1   Look out a 20 cm (8 in) round, loose-bottomed flan tin. Set the oven to 190C, 375F, Gas 5.
2   Lightly flour the work surface and roll out the pastry to a 25 cm (10 in) round. Roll the pastry round the rolling pin and unroll onto the tin. Line the tin, pressing the pastry into the dents, and level the top with a sharp knife. Prick the base with a fork, then cover with greaseproof paper and baking beans.
3   Bake for 10 minutes, remove the greaseproof paper and baking beans and bake for a further 5 minutes to dry out the base. Take out of the oven. Lower the heat to 170C, 340F, Gas 3.
4   Meanwhile, prepare the filling. Halve and stone the plums, then halve again. Crack the eggs into a mug and whisk lightly with a fork. Coarsely chop the chocolate into chunks. Very coarsely chop the whole almonds.
5   Put the butter and sugar in a mixing bowl and beat together until light and creamy. Gradually add the eggs, beating into the mixture a little at a time until light and fluffy. Stir in the ground almonds and chocolate.
6   Spoon the chocolate mixture over the bottom of the pastry case and level with the back of the spoon. Scatter the plums and chopped almonds evenly over the top.
7   Bake for 30 to 35 minutes or until just firm in the centre and golden brown all over. Leave to stand for 5 minutes before removing from the tin.

Cook's Tip
This is also good with fresh peaches or apricots, or try peeled, cored and sliced pears and replace the white chocolate with dark chocolate, 50% cocoa solids.

CHOCOLATE AND VANILLA FENCE

Time to make: 40 minutes
Time to bake: 8 minutes

Makes 20 cm (8 in) round border

6 medium eggs, size 3

200 g (8 oz) caster sugar

2 tablespoons hot water

1 teaspoon natural vanilla essence

125 g (5 oz) plain flour

25 g (1 oz) cocoa powder

Filling

200 g (8 oz) apricot preserve

2 tablespoons hot water

Topping

50 g (2 oz) milk chocolate

50 g (2 oz) good quality white chocolate

50 g (2 oz) dark chocolate, 50% cocoa solids

icing sugar to dust

Photographed on page 2

This is a striking sponge that's made by sandwiching a chocolate and a plain Swiss roll together. Fill it with a simple chocolate mousse (see following recipe), ice cream, cream whipped with coffee or liqueur, or a soft cheese and chopped fruit.

1   Look out two 33 x 23 cm (13 x 9 in) Swiss roll tins. Grease and line with greaseproof paper. Set the oven to 200C, 400F, Gas 6. Look out two large, wide-necked measuring jugs. Get ready two large sheets of greaseproof paper and sprinkle with caster sugar.
2   Crack the eggs into one of the jugs. Add the sugar and whisk with an electric whisk for 10 to 12 minutes or until the mixture is the colour and texture of whipped cream and leaves a trail when you pull out the beaters. Whisk in the water and vanilla essence.
3   Pour half of the mixture into the second jug. Put a sieve over one jug, add 75 g (3 oz) of the flour, sift then fold in gently with a metal spoon. Pour into one of the prepared Swiss roll tins.
4   Put the sieve over the remaining jug, add the remaining 50 g (2 oz) flour and the cocoa powder, sift then fold in gently with a metal spoon. Pour into the second Swiss roll tin.
5   Bake for 8 minutes or until the centre of each cake springs back when pressed and the mixture has shrunk from the sides of the tin. Turn out onto the greaseproof paper. Peel off the lining papers.
6   To make the filling: spoon the jam and water into a small non-stick pan and heat gently. Divide between the sponges. Stack the sponges on top of each other. Trim the edges.
7   Cut the cake in half parallel with the short sides and stack one half on top of the other. You should now have a stack of four layers of cake about 16 cm (6 in) wide. Cut this stack in four so that you have four strips about 4 cm (1½ in) wide.
8   Look out a 20 cm (8 in) round, deep, loose-bottomed cake tin. Divide the strips of cakes in four along the longest edge. (This will give you the height of the finished cake.) You should now have 16 piles of cake four layers high.
9   Arrange each pile of cake so that the sponges run vertically up the side of the tin and the cakes alternate chocolate and plain, all round the inside of the tin. Press each bundle of four tightly to the next to make as even an edge as you can.

10 Cover with a tea-towel and set aside while preparing the filling (see the following recipe).
11 To finish, shave off thick curls from the milk and white chocolate using a vegetable peeler and sprinkle over the cake.
12 Melt the dark chocolate in a microwave or over a pan of hot water. Pour into a piping bag fitted with a medium nozzle and pipe about six sets of three lines onto greaseproof paper. Leave to set slightly, then pipe three more lines across them to form a lattice. When set, carefully peel away the paper and arrange on the curls. Sprinkle with icing sugar and cut into wedges to serve.

THE ULTIMATE CHOCOLATE MOUSSE

Time to make: 20 minutes
Time to set: 4 hours

Makes enough filling for a sponge-lined 20 cm (8 in) round cake tin which will serve 8

250 g (9 oz) dark chocolate, 50% cocoa solids

300 ml (10 fl oz) double cream

1 tablespoon dark rum, optional

2 tablespoons glycerine or liquid glucose

4 egg whites

Using the Chocolate and Vanilla Fence to line a tin, this is a great and simple filling. Alternatively, pour the mousse into an 18 cm (7 in) round sandwich tin lined with non-pvc clear film. Sprinkle with chopped roasted hazelnuts, crushed amaretti or ginger biscuits. Leave to set. Serve in small portions – it's very rich.

1 Break the chocolate into squares and put in a non-stick pan with half of the cream. Add the rum, if using, and the glycerine or glucose. Heat gently, stirring well to mix, until the chocolate has melted. Remove from the heat.
2 Put the egg whites in a clean, grease-free bowl and whisk until they hold soft peaks.
3 Put the remaining cream in a small bowl and whip until it just holds its shape.
4 Pour the chocolate onto the egg whites and fold in gently with a metal spoon. Fold in the cream until blended. Pour into the centre of the Chocolate and Vanilla Fence and shake the tin to level the top. Chill for at least 4 hours or until firm. Carefully remove from the tin to a serving plate. Finish as described above.

WHITE CHOCOLATE CHEESECAKE

Time to make: 20 minutes
Time to bake: 30 minutes plus
  cooling time

Serves 8

Base

25 g (1 oz) unsalted butter

**100 g (4 oz) plain chocolate
digestive biscuits**

Filling

**250 g (8 oz) good quality white
chocolate**

**500 g (1 lb) full-fat soft cheese
or mascarpone**

**150 ml (5 fl oz) fresh soured
cream**

2 medium eggs, size 3

**½ teaspoon natural vanilla
essence**

This is the best cheesecake recipe I know and I am always being asked for the recipe. It is dense and creamy and tastes subtly of both cheese and chocolate. To serve: dust sparingly with icing sugar or pile lots of fresh fruit and white chocolate leaves on top. Serve with a fruity sauce of puréed strawberries, raspberries or mango.

1   Look out a 20 cm (8 in) round, deep, loose-bottomed cake tin. Set the oven to 170C, 340F, Gas 3.
2   To make the base: melt the butter in a small non-stick pan. Put the biscuits in a plastic bag and crush with a rolling pin. Add to the butter and mix together well.
3   Turn the mixture into the tin and press flat with a fork, making sure it spreads right to the edge. Chill while making the filling.
4   To make the filling: break the chocolate into pieces and melt in a microwave or over a pan of hot water. Put the cheese, soured cream and eggs in a bowl and mix briefly until just blended. Do not overbeat.
5   Stir in the melted chocolate and the vanilla essence and mix until well blended and smooth.
6   Spoon the mixture onto the biscuit base and level the top. Bake for 30 minutes or until the mixture feels firm for about 2.5 cm (1 in) around the edge but is still soft in the middle. Switch off the heat, leave the oven door slightly open and leave the cheesecake to cool. Chill before serving.

Cook's Tips
Try not to whisk air into the cheesecake. Beat the ingredients just enough to blend them. Too much air makes the cheesecake rise and sink or rise and crack. It is also important not to overcook the cheesecake or it goes grainy around the edge.
To make chocolate leaves, wash and dry rose leaves thoroughly. Melt some chocolate in a microwave or over a pan of hot water, then brush onto the underside of the leaves. Leave to set, then very carefully peel off the leaves.

CHOCOLATE ORANGE TRUFFLE CHEESECAKE

Time to make: 30 minutes
Time to bake: 30 minutes plus
   cooling time

Serves 8 to 10

Base

25 g (1 oz) unsalted butter

100 g (4 oz) gingernut biscuits

Filling

1 orange

250 g (8 oz) dark chocolate, 50% cocoa solids

500 g (1 lb) full-fat soft cheese or mascarpone

150 ml (5 fl oz) fresh soured cream

2 medium eggs, size 3

100 g (4 oz) good quality white chocolate

D ark, dense and intense with a smooth, truffle-like texture, this cheesecake is best served at room temperature.

1 Look out a 20 cm (8 in) round, deep, loose-bottomed cake tin. Set the oven to 170C, 340F, Gas 3.
2 To make the base: melt the butter in a small non-stick pan. Put the biscuits in a plastic bag and crush with a rolling pin. Add the biscuits to the butter and mix together well.
3 Turn the mixture into the tin and press flat with a fork, making sure it spreads right to the edge. Chill while making the filling.
4 To make the filling: finely grate the rind from the orange. Break the dark chocolate into pieces and melt in a microwave or over a pan of hot water. Put the orange rind, cheese, soured cream and eggs in a bowl and mix briefly until just blended. Do not overbeat.
5 Stir in the melted chocolate and mix until well blended and smooth.
6 Spoon the mixture onto the biscuit base and level the top.
7 Break the white chocolate into pieces and melt in a microwave or over a pan of hot water. Pour into the dark chocolate mixture, stirring lightly so that the chocolate stays marbled.
8 Bake for 30 minutes or until the mixture feels firm for about 2.5 cm (1 in) around the edge but is still soft in the middle. Switch off the heat, leave the oven door slightly open and leave the cheesecake to cool. Chill before serving.

CHOCOLATE, PECAN AND MAPLE PIE

Time to make: 25 minutes
Time to bake: 45 minutes

Serves 8

375 g (13 oz) packet sweet shortcrust pastry

150 g (6 oz) dark chocolate, 50% cocoa solids

50 g (2 oz) unsalted butter

2 tablespoons pure maple syrup

1 teaspoon natural vanilla essence

4 medium eggs, size 3

150 g (6 oz) pecan nuts

To finish

3 tablespoons pure maple syrup

I am not a great lover of chocolate and short pastry together but this is one of the exceptions. This pie has a thin chocolate custard, a crust of sweet pecans and a shiny maple syrup top. The flavours and textures work brilliantly together and I serve it warm with whipped cream or vanilla ice cream and hand round extra maple syrup to pour on top.

1   Look out a 20 cm (8 in) fluted, loose-bottomed flan tin. Set the oven to 200C, 400F, Gas 6
2   Lightly flour the work surface and roll out the pastry to a 25 cm (10 in) round. Roll the pastry round the rolling pin and unroll onto the tin. Line the tin, pressing the pastry into the dents, and level the top with a sharp knife. Prick the base with a fork then cover with greaseproof paper and baking beans.
3   Bake for 10 minutes; remove the greaseproof paper and baking beans and bake for a further 5 minutes to dry out the base. Take out of the oven and set aside. Lower the heat to 180C, 350F, Gas 4.
4   Break the chocolate into pieces and put in a small non-stick pan with the butter. Heat gently until melted. Remove from the heat and add the maple syrup and vanilla essence.
5   Crack the eggs into a mug and beat lightly. Set aside 30 pecan nuts for the top; chop the rest.
6   Add the eggs and chopped nuts to the chocolate mixture and stir well to mix. Pour into the pastry case.
7   Arrange the reserved pecan nuts neatly in three circles starting at the outside edge. Bake for 30 minutes or until the pastry is golden and the mixture feels firm in the centre. Leave to cool.
8   To finish: brush the top with maple syrup, then cut into wedges to serve.

Cook's Tip
Pure maple syrup is much more expensive than its synthetic imitations, but the flavour is really worth it. It keeps for ages.

BECCA'S BEST EVER CHOCOLATE TRUFFLE CAKE

Time to make: 20 minutes plus
    chilling time
Time to bake: 8 to 10 minutes

Serves 8 to 10

Sponge

2 medium eggs, size 3

50 g (2 oz) caster sugar

2 tablespoons cocoa powder

¼ teaspoon ground cinnamon

Truffle

425 g (15 oz) dark chocolate, 50% cocoa solids

600 ml (20 fl oz) double cream

2 tablespoons orange-flavoured liqueur

Topping

200 g (8 oz) good quality white chocolate

icing sugar, to dust

My friend Becca has worked on and off in restaurants throughout her career, collecting recipes as she goes. A fellow chocolate lover, she says that after years of eating chocolate pudding this is the best truffle cake ever. Don't take her word for it – try it yourself! Cut into thin wedges and serve with black coffee or serve with coffee- or ginger-flavoured cream and fresh orange segments.

1 Look out a 20 cm (8 in) round, loose-bottomed cake tin. Grease and line with greaseproof paper. Set the oven to 200C, 400F, Gas 6.
2 To make the sponge: crack the eggs into a mixing bowl, add the sugar and whisk with an electric whisk for 5 minutes until the mixture is the colour and texture of whipped cream. Put a sieve over the bowl, add the cocoa and cinnamon, sift then fold in with a metal spoon.
3 Pour the mixture into the prepared tin and bake for 8 to 10 minutes or until the mixture shrinks from the side of the tin. Leave to cool in the tin.
4 To make the truffle: break the chocolate into pieces and melt in a microwave or over a pan of hot water. Put the cream and the liqueur in a large bowl and whip until it just holds its shape. Pour in the warm chocolate and whisk until smooth.
5 Pour the chocolate mixture over the sponge and level the top. Chill for at least 5 hours or overnight until completely firm.
6 Very carefully remove from the tin, peel off the lining paper and place on a serving plate. Decorate with large rolls of white chocolate scrolls (see below). Sprinkle with icing sugar.

Cook's Tip
To make amazing white chocolate scrolls like those in the photograph, melt the white chocolate in a microwave or over a pan of hot water, then spread it thinly on a marble slab. Leave at room temperature until it has set but is not so cold that it becomes brittle. Using a paint scraper held at a slight angle to the chocolate, push it away from you to make scrolls.

CHOCOLATE TRUFFLE ICE CREAM

Time to make: 10 minutes
Time to chill: 4 hours

Makes 1 litre (1¼ pints)

300 g (10 oz) of your favourite milk chocolate

300 ml (10 fl oz) double cream

400 g or 350 ml (14 oz or 12 fl oz) tub bought vanilla custard made with double cream

This ice cream needs time to come to before serving, so take it out of the freezer before you sit down to your main course. It has a creamy and luxurious texture and a good chocolate flavour. Don't be tempted to replace the milk chocolate with something like a 70% cocoa solids dark chocolate because I've tried it and the texture goes brittle.

1 Break the chocolate into pieces and melt in a microwave or over a pan of hot water.
2 Whip the cream until it just holds its shape. Whisk in the custard, then whisk in the chocolate until the mixture is well blended.
3 Pour the mixture into a 1.4 litre (2 pt) freezer-proof container and freeze for 4 hours or until firm.
4 To serve: remove from the freezer and leave to stand at room temperature for 10 minutes.

Cook's Tip
If you are in a hurry this ice cream defrosts well in the microwave. Give it 30 seconds on defrost (30% power) then test with your fingers to see if it has softened enough to scoop. Repeat until it is ready.

ALMOND CRUNCH
Roughly crush 6 standard size Dime® bars and fold into the mixture at the end of step 2.

DARK CHOCOLATE AND MINT
Replace the milk chocolate with dark chocolate, 50% cocoa solids. Break 100 g (4 oz) – about half a box – of After Eight® mints into small pieces. Fold into the mixture at the end of step 2.

WHITE CHOCOLATE ICE CREAM

Time to make: 10 minutes
Time to chill: 4 hours

Makes 1 litre (1¾ pints)

300 g (10 oz) good quality white chocolate

300 ml (10 fl oz) double cream

400 g or 350 ml (14 oz or 12 fl oz) tub bought vanilla custard made with double cream

This recipe makes a truly wonderful soft-scoop ice cream with an intensely white chocolate flavour. I use it as a base for all sorts of variations and would say it is one of my best inventions!

1 Break the chocolate into pieces and melt in a microwave or over a pan of hot water.
2 Whip the cream until it just holds its shape. Whisk in the custard then whisk in the chocolate until the mixture is well blended.
3 Pour the mixture into a 1.4 litre (2 pt) freezer-proof container and freeze for 4 hours or until firm.
4 To serve: remove from the freezer and leave to stand at room temperature for 10 minutes.

TOFFEE RIPPLE
Put 150 g (5 oz) bought toffee bars in a small non-stick pan with 150 ml (5 fl oz) double cream and heat gently until melted. Leave to cool to room temperature. Pour onto the ice cream mixture before it is frozen, but do not stir in – allow the toffee to marble the ice cream. Freeze until firm.

COOKIES AND CREAM

Time to make: 15 minutes
Time to chill: 4 hours

Makes 1 litre (1¾ pints)

1 quantity White Chocolate Ice Cream (see above), made up to the end of step 2

100 g (4 oz) Oreo® cookies or chocolate bourbon biscuits

American Oreo® cookies are two dark cocoa-flavoured rounds sandwiched with a firm white buttercream. You can buy them here from American specialist shops, but they are horribly expensive. A chocolate bourbon makes a thrifty (and good) substitute.

1 Put the biscuits in a bowl and crush roughly with the end of a rolling pin. Fold into the white chocolate mixture.
2 Pour the mixture into a 1. 4 litre (2 pt) freezer-proof container and freeze for 4 hours or until firm.
3 To serve: remove from the freezer and leave to stand at room temperature for 10 minutes.

ITALIAN MOCHA CHARLOTTE

Time to make: 35 minutes
Time to chill: 4 hours

Serves 4 to 6

Filling

300 g (10 oz) dark chocolate, 50% cocoa solids

3 medium eggs, size 3

25 g (1 oz) caster sugar

25 g (1 oz) unsalted butter, at room temperature

25 g (1 oz) walnut pieces

Outside

1 teaspoon instant coffee granules

3 tablespoons boiling water

125 g (5 oz) sponge fingers

To finish

½ teaspoon cocoa powder

coffee bean shaped chocolates

½ teaspoon icing sugar

This recipe comes from my Auntie Elma who is a very good cook. At family gatherings, we all used to check the buffet table to see if her famous Charlotte was there. As a professional, hers was always done in a proper Charlotte tin, designed to be exactly sponge finger height and with sides that slope out slightly, and was big enough to satisfy the MacLennan clan. My version is of more modest proportions and done in a pudding basin.

1   Look out a 1 litre (1¾ pt) pudding basin with a sloping side.
2   To make the filling: break the chocolate into squares and melt in a microwave or over a pan of hot water. Separate the eggs: put the yolks in a mixing bowl and whites in a clean, grease-free bowl.
3   Add the sugar to the egg yolks and whisk together with an electric whisk for 5 minutes until the mixture is pale and creamy. Add the butter and melted chocolate and whisk together for 1 minute until the mixture is smooth and light.
4   Whisk the egg whites until they hold soft peaks. Fold into the chocolate mixture using a metal spoon. Spoon just enough mixture into the basin to cover the base.
5   To prepare the outside: dissolve the coffee in the water on a teaplate with a rim. Briefly dip in the sponge fingers, one at a time, flat side down. Arrange upright around the inside of the basin, with the dipped side facing in, on top of the chocolate mixture. Cut up remaining fingers to fill the gaps.
6   Pour half of the remaining chocolate mixture into the basin and scatter the walnuts on top. Cover with the remaining mixture and smooth the top. Chill for 4 hours or until firm.
7   To finish: turn out the charlotte onto a serving plate. Dust the top with cocoa powder and decorate with coffee bean shaped chocolates. Sprinkle with icing sugar. Cut into thin wedges to serve.

Cook's Tip
Choose an old-fashioned pudding basin with a straight sloping side. The new basins, although the same size, are too rounded.

CHOCOLATE GINGERNUT LOG

Time to make: 15 minutes
Time to chill: 4 hours

Serves 8

150 g (6 oz) gingernut biscuits

300 g (10 oz) dark chocolate, 50% cocoa solids

4 tablespoons double cream

4 medium eggs, size 3

This log cuts really well to show a dark chocolate mousse with sweet pockets of softened ginger biscuits in it. Serve with single cream flavoured with grated orange rind, or whipped cream with 2 tablespoons of the syrup from a stem ginger jar folded through it.

1   Look out a 450 g (1 lb) loaf tin and line with non-pvc clear film. Break the gingernut biscuits roughly into about 6 bits each and put in a bowl.
2   Break the chocolate into pieces and melt in a microwave or over a pan of hot water. Stir in the cream.
3   Separate the eggs: put the yolks in a mug and the whites in a large, clean, grease-free bowl. Add the yolks to the chocolate and beat until the mixture is thick and shiny. Whisk the egg whites until they hold soft peaks. Fold into the chocolate mixture.
4   Stir in the biscuits, mixing well. Turn the mixture into the prepared tin and level the top with the back of a spoon. Cover with non-pvc clear film and chill for at least 4 hours or until set.
5   To serve: uncover the tin and invert onto a serving plate. Peel off the clear film. Cut into 8 even slices to serve.

Cook's Tip
This log improves with keeping and cuts better the day after it is made. Try adding 25 g (1 oz) sultanas warmed in a saucepan with 2 tablespoons dark rum until they are plump. Cover and cool and add at the end of step 3.

QUICK CAPPUCCINO MOUSSE

Time to make: 15 minutes
Time to chill: 1 hour

Makes 4

100 g (4 oz) dark chocolate, 50% cocoa solids

knob of butter

2 medium eggs, size 3

2 teaspoons coffee-flavoured liqueur

6 tablespoons whipping cream

pinch of drinking chocolate powder

I think this combination of eggs and chocolate makes a very simple, can't-fail mousse with a glorious texture. If you ever have friends round for supper during the week, this is one of those recipes that you can mix up when you get home from work and by the time you clear away the main course, it is ready to serve.

1 Look out four after-dinner size coffee cups.
2 Break the chocolate into squares and melt in a microwave or over a pan of hot water. Add the butter and stir until it has melted. Allow to stand.
3 Separate the eggs: place the yolks in a mug and the whites in a clean, grease-free bowl. Whisk the whites until they hold soft peaks.
4 Add the egg yolks and liqueur to the chocolate mixture, stirring until smooth, thick and shiny. Fold in the egg whites with a metal spoon until there is no white left.
5 Pour into the coffee cups and chill for 1 hour or until set.
6 To serve: lightly whip the cream until it just thickens and holds its shape. Pile on top of the mousses, swirling right to the rim of the cups. Sprinkle with drinking chocolate, place on a saucer and serve with a coffee spoon.

MUM'S UNCOOKED CHOCOLATE CHERRY CAKE

Time to make: 25 minutes
Time to chill: 6 hours or
   overnight

Serves 12 to 16

100 g (4 oz) glacé or
maraschino cherries

200 g (8 oz) dark chocolate,
50% cocoa solids

200 g (8 oz) unsalted butter

150 g (6 oz) plain biscuits
(like Rich Tea)

100 g (4 oz) walnut pieces

2 teaspoons instant coffee
granules

1 tablespoon hot water

100 g (4 oz) caster sugar

3 medium eggs, size 3

My Mum has guarded this recipe for years. It was part of our Christmas tradition, was made for birthdays and, once we had all left home, as a special pudding when we went to visit at weekends. It has a rich, fudge-like texture with chunks of biscuit and sweet cherries. It cuts like a dream and keeps well in the fridge for up to a week. The walnuts are my addition.

1 Look out an 18 cm (7 in) round, deep, loose-bottomed cake tin and line with non-pvc clear film, leaving some overhanging the edge.
2 Rinse the cherries and pat dry with absorbent kitchen paper. Break the chocolate into pieces and put in a non-stick pan with the butter. Heat gently, stirring occasionally, until melted. Remove from the heat.
3 Put the biscuits in a mixing bowl and break into rough chunks with the end of a rolling pin. Add the walnut pieces and cherries and mix together.
4 Spoon the coffee into a large mixing bowl. Add the water and stir to dissolve. Add the sugar and eggs and beat with an electric whisk until the mixture is light and creamy.
5 Whisk the warm melted chocolate into the egg mixture until smooth and shiny. Fold in the biscuit mixture and stir well until everything is coated with chocolate.
6 Pour the mixture into the prepared tin and shake the tin so the mixture runs right to the edge. Chill for at least 6 hours or overnight.
7 To serve: pull the cake out of the tin using the clear film. Peel off the clear film and slide the cake onto a serving plate or small marble slab. Don't cut into wedges, instead cut into finger-thick slices.

Cook's Tip
You can prick the top of the cake in several places with a skewer and pour over a couple of spoons of your favourite spirit or liqueur before chilling. Choose one that is sympathetic to the flavours of the cake, such as orange, coffee, dark rum or brandy.

CREAMY CHOCOLATE CAKE

Time to make: 25 minutes
Time to bake: 30 minutes

Serves 6 to 8

200 g (8 oz) dark chocolate, 50% cocoa solids

150 ml (5 fl oz) double cream

3 medium eggs, size 3

50 g (2 oz) icing sugar

1 tablespoon cornflour

25 g (1 oz) cocoa powder

icing sugar to dust

This is a simple baked cake that is somewhere in texture between a creamy custard and a velvety mousse.

1 Look out an 18 cm (7 in) round, deep, loose-bottomed cake tin. Grease and line with greaseproof paper. Set the oven to 170C, 340F, Gas 3.

2 Break the chocolate into pieces and melt in a micowave or over a pan of hot water. Whip the cream until it just holds its shape.

3 Crack the eggs into a large measuring jug. Put a sieve over the jug, add the icing sugar, cornflour and cocoa powder and sift in. Whisk with an electric mixer for 5 minutes or until thick, frothy and doubled in volume.

4 Stir in the melted chocolate and fold in the whipped cream. Pour the mixture into the prepared tin and level the top.

5 Bake for 30 minutes. Leave to cool in the tin, then transfer to a wire rack and peel off the lining paper. Dust the cake lightly with sifted icing sugar and leave to cool completely. Cut into wedges to serve.

Cook's Tip
Try dipping fruits in melted dark chocolate to serve with desserts – gooseberries, strawberries and cherries look especially stunning.

FUDGE BROWNIE PIE

Time to make: 25 minutes
Time to bake: 30 to 35 minutes

Serves 6

200 g (8 oz) digestive biscuits

50 g (2 oz) butter

Filling

150 g (6 oz) dark chocolate, 50% cocoa solids

100 g (4 oz) butter

200 g (8 oz) caster sugar

1 teaspoon natural vanilla essence

2 medium eggs, size 3

50 g (2 oz) plain flour

Topping

150 ml (5 fl oz) whipping cream

50 g (2 oz) bar chunky chocolate

We eat outdoors as often as the weather allows and Sunday lunch is often a picnic or barbecue with friends. When the sun's out I want maximum fresh air and minimum fuss in the kitchen. This pudding has become a bit of trademark, eagerly devoured by grown-ups and children, and ideal for casual entertaining. It has a crisp biscuit base, a sticky chocolate brownie middle and a swirl of cream and more chocolate on top.

1   Look out a 23 cm (9 in) pie plate or flan dish and line the base with greaseproof paper. Set the oven to 170C, 340F, Gas 3. Put the biscuits in a large plastic bag and crush them with a rolling pin. Put the butter in a small non-stick pan and heat gently until melted. Add the biscuit crumbs and stir well to mix.
2   Pile the biscuit mixture into the pie plate or flan dish and spread over the base and side. Press with the back of a spoon to make an even layer.
3   For the filling: break the chocolate into squares, put in a small non-stick pan with the butter and sugar and heat gently, stirring, until smooth. Remove from the heat and stir in the vanilla essence.
4   Crack the eggs into a mug and beat with a fork, then beat into the mixture. Put a sieve over the pan, add the flour, sift then stir gently into the mixture.
5   Pour into the pie plate or flan dish and bake for 30 to 35 minutes or until the filling is just firm in the centre. Leave to cool to room temperature.
6   To finish, pour the cream into a bowl and whip lightly until it just holds its shape. Pile onto the pie and swirl to cover the top. Hold a grater over the pie and grate the chocolate coarsely over the top. Cut into wedges to serve.

Cook's Tip
This pie is good warm too, in which case let it cool for 5 minutes once it's out of the oven, cut into wedges and offer the cream and grated chocolate separately.

CHOCOLATE MERINGUE TOWER

Time to make: 25 minutes
Time to bake: 1 to 1½ hours plus
  2 to 4 hours standing time

Serves 8

Meringue

50 g (2 oz) cocoa powder

100 g (4 oz) icing sugar

6 egg whites

pinch of salt

175 g (7 oz) caster sugar

Filling

200 g (8 oz) good quality white chocolate

150 ml (5 fl oz) single cream

200 g (8 oz) fresh raspberries

icing sugar to dust

chocolate leaves (optional)

I love puddings that friends gasp at when they see them. This is one.

1 Look out two large flat baking sheets and line with non-stick baking parchment. On one sheet draw a 5 cm (2 in) circle and a 20 cm (8 in) circle. On the other sheet, draw a 10 cm (4 in) circle and a 15 cm (6 in) circle. Set the oven to 150C, 300F, Gas 1.
2 To make the meringue: put a sieve over a wide-necked measuring jug. Add the cocoa powder and icing sugar and sift into the jug.
3 Put the egg whites in a large, clean, grease-free bowl and whisk until very stiff. Add the salt and a spoonful of the caster sugar and whisk well. Continue adding the caster sugar, a spoonful at a time, whisking well between each addition. Sift cocoa powder mixture over the egg white mixture and fold in gently with a metal spoon.
4 Divide the mixture between the circles, spreading it to the edges. (Alternatively, spoon the mixture into a piping bag fitted with a large plain nozzle.)
5 Cut the paper between the largest and the smallest circle so that you can take the smallest circle out first. Bake the meringues for 1 hour. Remove the smallest one and bake the rest for a further 30 minutes. Leave to cool.
6 To make the filling: break the chocolate into pieces and put in a small non-stick pan. Add the cream and heat gently, stirring until the chocolate has melted. Remove from the heat and beat to make a smooth, glossy, spreadable mixture. Divide the mixture between the meringues and spread to the edges.
7 Place the largest meringue on a flat serving plate. Cover with raspberries and top with the next largest meringue. Repeat, finishing with raspberries on top of the smallest meringue.
8 Leave to stand for 2 to 4 hours. Dust lightly with icing sugar and decorate with chocolate leaves if liked (see page 30) to serve.

Cook's Tip
To cut this into 8 portions: remove the top two meringues and cut into three wedges. Then cut the bottom two meringues into 5 wedges.

WHITE CHOCOLATE AND GINGER BRÛLÉE

Time to make: 15 minutes
Time to bake: 20 to 25 minutes

Makes 4

2 round pieces stem ginger in syrup

4 egg yolks, medium size 3

100 g (4 oz) good quality white chocolate

300 ml (10 fl oz) double cream

These are foolproof, easy and melt-in-the-mouth. My Mum suggested adding the ginger and it works really well.

1 Set the oven to 170C, 340F, Gas 3. Look out 4 small ramekins. Finely chop the ginger. Put the egg yolks in a large measuring jug.
2 Break the chocolate into pieces and put in a small non-stick pan with the cream. Heat gently, stirring occasionally until the chocolate has melted, then bring to the boil.
3 Pour the cream mixture onto the egg yolks, whisking all the time, then return to the pan and heat for 1 to 2 minutes, stirring constantly. Do not boil. Remove from the heat.
4 Divide the mixture evenly between the ramekins and add a quarter of the chopped ginger to each. It will sink to the bottom.
5 Bake for 20 to 25 minutes until set. Remove from the oven and leave to cool completely. Chill before serving.

Cook's Tip
Use the egg whites to make meringues, see Chocolate Meringue Tower on page 46, or label and freeze.

DARK VELVET BRÛLÉE

Time to make: 10 minutes
Time to bake: 10 to 15 minutes

Makes 4

4 egg yolks

100 g (4 oz) dark chocolate, 70% cocoa solids

300 ml (10 fl oz) double cream

75 g (3 oz) caster sugar

I'm really not a great custard fan but these are silky with chocolate, rich and dark with a crisp, crunchy top. They are ideal for entertaining because they can be made in advance.

1 Set the oven to 170C, 340F, Gas 3. Look out 4 small ramekins. Put the egg yolks in a large measuring jug.
2 Break the chocolate into pieces and put in a small non-stick pan with the cream. Heat gently, stirring occasionally, until the chocolate has melted, then bring to the boil.
3 Pour the cream mixture onto the egg yolks, whisking all the time, then return to the pan and heat for 1 to 2 minutes, stirring constantly. Do not boil. Remove the pan from the heat.
4 Divide the mixture evenly between the ramekins and bake for 10 to 15 minutes until set. Leave to cool completely.
5 Turn the grill to its highest setting. Arrange the ramekins on a baking sheet and sprinkle the sugar evenly over the top of the chocolate custards. When the grill is really hot, flash the ramekins under it for 30 seconds to 1 minute or until the sugar browns and bubbles. Chill before serving.

JENNY'S CHOCOLATE TRUFFLES

Time to make: 20 minutes

Makes 24

100 g (4 oz) dark chocolate, 50% cocoa solids

100 g (4 oz) milk chocolate

2 egg yolks from free-range eggs

1 tablespoon thick Greek-style natural yogurt

1 tablespoon Cointreau or other liqueur

1 tablespoon icing sugar

2 tablespoons cocoa powder

These have a thick fudgy texture and a subtle hint of orange. Great after dinner with a cup of coffee instead of a pudding or as a decoration on a special cake.

1 Break the chocolate into pieces and melt in a microwave or over a pan of hot water.
2 Add the egg yolks, yogurt and liqueur and stir well to mix. Cool to room temperature then chill until stiff enough to handle.
3 Mix the icing sugar and cocoa powder together and sift onto a plate.
4 Scoop out the mixture with a teaspoon and roll into 24 balls. Roll each truffle in the cocoa powder mixture.
5 Store in the fridge for up to three days until required.

Biscuits and cookies

There's nothing ordinary or everyday about these recipes. The cookies are melt-in-the mouth, the florentines a wonderful blend of toffee and nut flavours, the shortbreads and the melt-and-mix biscuit bar as easy as they come. And then there's the biscuits with pepper, chilli and spices.

FOUR-NUT FLORENTINES

Time to make: 15 minutes
Time to bake: 10 to 12 minutes

Makes 18

**200 g (8 oz) bag natural,
shelled mixed nuts (Brazil nuts,
walnuts, hazelnuts and
almonds)**

75 g (3 oz) butter

100 g (4 oz) icing sugar

4 tablespoons milk

40 g (1½ oz) plain flour

To finish

**150 g (6 oz) dark chocolate,
50% cocoa solids**

**50 g (2 oz) good quality white
chocolate**

Just before Christmas, I came across a bag of mixed, shelled, unsalted nuts in the crisps and nibbles section of the supermarket. I thought they would be handy for some of the traditional pies, puddings and cakes but they ended up in these wonderful, crisp, toffee-flavoured biscuits instead.

1   Look out two large baking sheets and line with non-stick baking parchment. Set the oven to 170C, 340F, Gas 3. Roughly chop the nuts.
2   Put the butter in a small non-stick pan and add the icing sugar and milk. Heat gently until the butter has melted, then whisk well to make a smooth, shiny but cloudy mixture.
3   Put a sieve over the pan, add the flour then sift in. Add the nuts and stir well to mix.
4   Measure 9 spoonsful of the mixture onto each baking sheet, leaving plenty of space between them.
5   Bake for 10 to 12 minutes or until the edges look lacy and are golden brown. Leave to cool for 10 minutes then transfer to a wire rack.
6   To finish: break the chocolate into pieces and melt in separate bowls in a microwave or over a pan of hot water. Turn the biscuits over and spread the dark chocolate in an even layer on the base of each. Drizzle the white chocolate over from the tip of a teaspoon and marble into the dark chocolate using a cocktail stick. Leave to set for 30 minutes. Store in an airtight tin.

Cook's Tips
The biscuits are very soft when they come out of the oven but they crisp as they cool. Handle them carefully when you lift them off the baking sheet.
If you are making a big batch of these – say for Christmas presents or the school cake sale – as one batch cools and is transferred to the wire rack, re-use the baking parchment for the next batch.

GINGER AND ORANGE FLORENTINES

Time to make: 20 minutes
Time to bake: 10 to 12 minutes

Makes 18

75 g (3 oz) good quality candied orange peel

75 g (3 oz) crystallized ginger

75 g (3 oz) glacé pineapple

75 g (3 oz) blanched whole almonds

½ small orange

75 g (3 oz) butter

100 g (4 oz) icing sugar

4 tablespoons milk

40 g (1½ oz) plain flour

To finish

150 g (6 oz) good quality white chocolate

I usually make a light Christmas cake using dried pineapple, citrus peels, apricots, almonds and ginger. I had some ingredients left over last year so this recipe came about. I prefer this tropical fruit and nut mixture to the traditional blend of almonds, cherries and citrus peel. They taste good with dark chocolate bottoms, too.

1 Look out two large baking sheets and line with non-stick baking parchment. Set the oven to 190C, 375F, Gas 5.
2 Roughly chop the candied peel, ginger, pineapple and almonds. Coarsely grate the rind from the orange.
3 Put the butter in a small non-stick pan and add the icing sugar and milk. Heat gently until the butter has melted, then whisk well to make a smooth, shiny but cloudy mixture.
4 Put a sieve over the pan, add the flour then sift in. Add the peel, ginger, pineapple, almonds and orange rind and stir well to mix.
5 Measure 9 spoonsful of the mixture onto each baking sheet, leaving plenty of space between them.
6 Bake for 10 to 12 minutes or until the edges look lacy and are golden brown. Leave to cool for 10 minutes, then transfer to a wire rack.
7 To finish: break the chocolate into pieces and melt in a microwave or over a pan of hot water. Turn the biscuits over and spread the chocolate in an even layer on the base of each. Draw wavy lines with a fork across the chocolate. Leave to set for 30 minutes. Store in an airtight tin.

Cook's Tip
These biscuits are best eaten within two days while they are still crisp. Any biscuits which go soft are great stirred into the White Chocolate Ice Cream on page 37 before freezing.

STEM GINGER SHORTBREADS WITH DARK CHOCOLATE CLOAKS

Time to make: 20 minutes
Time to bake: 20 minutes

Makes 12

375 g (13 oz) plain flour
250 g (9 oz) unsalted butter
125 g (5 oz) caster sugar
100 g (4 oz) crystallized ginger
100 g (4 oz) dark chocolate, 50% cocoa solids

These make lovely gifts – the sort of thing your granny would like as a special biscuit to have with her afternoon tea. Mine did, only she didn't think there was enough ginger in them so I've doubled my original amount and she says they are much better now. They are also good to serve with fools and flummeries and fruity fromage frais – especially the lemon one.

1 Look out two baking sheets. Set the oven to 150C, 300F, Gas 1.
2 Put a sieve over a food processor bowl, add the flour then sift in. Cut the butter into 8 or 9 pieces and add to the bowl. Process until the mixture just resembles breadcrumbs.
3 Add the sugar and process again until the mixture just begins to stick together into crumbles. Do not over-mix. (The dough should not begin to form a ball like pastry would.)
4 Turn the crumbly mixture out onto a work surface and knead lightly until it begins to bind together.
5 Finely chop the ginger and knead it in. Divide the mixture in half.
6 Lightly flour the work surface and roll each half into a 15 cm (6 in) round. Place each round on a baking sheet and mark into 6 triangles through the centre of the round.
7 Bake for 20 minutes or until pale golden on top and crisp on the bottom. Cut through the markings to separate the triangles and leave to cool.
8 Transfer to a wire rack with a baking sheet placed underneath. Melt the chocolate in a microwave or over a pan of hot water and pour over each shortbread. Leave to set, then store in an airtight tin.

WHITE CHOCOLATE SHORTCAKE

Time to make: 20 minutes
Time to bake: 30 minutes

Makes 9 pieces

150 g (6 oz) good quality white chocolate

225 g (9 oz) plain flour

150 g (6 oz) unsalted butter

75 g (3 oz) icing sugar

This recipe tastes more like a Dutch shortcake than a Scottish shortbread. It has a melt-in-the mouth texture and the white chocolate caramelizes slowly into golden chunks.

1 Look out an 18 cm (7 in) square cake tin. Set the oven to 150C, 300F, Gas 1. Chop the chocolate into rough chunks.
2 Put a sieve over a food processor bowl, add the flour then sift in. Cut the butter into 8 or 9 pieces and add to the bowl. Process until the mixture just resembles breadcrumbs.
3 Sift in the icing sugar and process again until the mixture just begins to stick together into crumbles. Do not over-mix.
(The dough should not begin to form a ball like pastry would.)
4 Turn the crumbly mixture out onto a work surface and knead lightly until it begins to bind together.
5 Scatter the chocolate on the work surface and knead it in.
6 Lightly press the mixture into the tin, rolling it flat with a jar. Mark it into 9 squares.
7 Bake for 30 minutes or until pale golden on top and crisp on the bottom. Cut through the markings to separate the squares.
8 Lift out of the tin with a palette knife and cool on a wire rack. Store in an airtight tin.

COCONUT OATIE BISCUITS

Time to make: 15 minutes
Time to bake: 15 minutes

Makes 12

---

100 g (4 oz) **butter or margarine**

100 g (4 oz) **self-raising flour**

75 g (3 oz) **Scottish porridge oats**

75 g (3 oz) **flaked or desiccated coconut**

200 g (8 oz) **soft light brown sugar**

1 tablespoon **clear honey**

2 tablespoons **boiling water**

Topping

100 g (4 oz) **dark chocolate, 50% cocoa solids**

25 g (1 oz) **butter**

Everyone who tasted these said they are very more-ish. The biscuit is sweet and slightly chewy and the dark chocolate is the perfect complement to the sweet oaty topping.

1   Look out a 20 cm (8 in) square, loose-bottomed cake tin and grease lightly. Set the oven to 170C, 340F, Gas 3.
2   Melt the butter or margarine in a large, non-stick pan. Add the flour, oats, coconut, sugar, honey and water and stir so that everything is well mixed.
3   Turn the mixture into the prepared tin and press down with a fork to make an even layer, pressing right to the edges.
4   Bake for 15 minutes or until golden. Remove from the oven, but leave in the tin.
5   To finish: put the chocolate and butter in a non-stick pan and heat gently until melted. Spread evenly over the top of the baked mixture. Leave to set, then cut into 12 squares.

Variation
Replace the honey and water with 1 medium egg, size 3. Divide the mixture into 18 pieces and roll into balls. Arrange well apart on two baking sheets and bake for 10 to 12 minutes. Leave to cool on the baking sheet, then cover the base of the biscuits with melted chocolate. Leave to set.

CHUNKY BISCUIT BAR

Time to make: 25 minutes, plus setting time

Makes about 20

---

300 g (10 oz) **milk chocolate**

200 g (8 oz) **shortcake biscuits**

100 g (4 oz) **sultanas**

---

1   Look out a 6 in (15 cm) square cake tin. Break the chocolate into pieces and melt in a microwave or in a non-stick pan over a low heat.
2   Roughly chop the biscuits and add to the chocolate with the sultanas. Stir well so that everything is well coated.
3   Pile the mixture into the tin and level the top with the back of a spoon. Chill until the chocolate has set. Cut into small squares.

PEAR AND GINGER BARS

Time to make: 20 minutes plus
setting time

Makes 10

**200 g (8 oz) dark chocolate,
50% cocoa solids**

250 g (9 oz) dried pear halves

75 g (3 oz) crystallized ginger

75 g (3 oz) sultana bran flakes

**good pinch of ground
cinnamon**

My close friend Mitzie is a great baker and she loves to experiment. When we go round to visit she always has something interesting in the cake tin to offer with a cup of coffee. These are rich, dark and sticky and I'm pleased to include them in my book. Cut into tiny squares they would also make a lovely gift as a slightly healthier alternative to a box of chocolates.

1 Look out a 33 x 25 cm (13 x 10 in) Swiss roll tin and line with non-stick baking parchment.
2 Break the chocolate into pieces and melt in a microwave or over a pan of hot water. Spread half of the chocolate over half the length of the tin.
3 Put the pears, ginger, bran flakes and cinnamon in a food processor and process until they are very finely chopped.
4 Spread the mixture evenly over the chocolate, pressing flat with a palette knife. Cover with the remaining chocolate, spreading evenly and smoothly.
5 Cover with the other half of the baking parchment and leave to cool. Before the chocolate has completely set, cut into bars.

Cook's Tip
Keep these in a container in the fridge for up to one week. Don't worry if the chocolate develops a white bloom – it is the cocoa butter coming to the surface and it won't affect the taste.

DOUBLE NUT AND WHITE CHOCOLATE COOKIES

Time to make: 25 minutes
Time to bake: about 10 minutes

Makes about 20

1 small egg, size 5
100 g (4 oz) Macadamia nuts
200 g (8 oz) good quality white chocolate
200 g (8 oz) sunflower margarine
50 g (2 oz) caster sugar
100 g (4 oz) soft light brown sugar
2 teaspoons natural vanilla essence
300 g (10 oz) plain flour
1 level teaspoon baking powder
75 g (3 oz) flaked coconut or toasted desiccated coconut

Made with coconut and waxy round Macadamias, these are my joint favourite cookies in the whole world. Inspired by those on sale at my nearest American cookie stall in the big shopping centre near home, I think they are sensational. Warm each cookie through for a few seconds in the microwave before you eat it if you like, so that the white chocolate starts to melt.

1   Line two baking sheets with non-stick baking parchment. Set the oven to 170C, 340F, Gas 3. Crack the egg into a mug and whisk lightly with a fork. Coarsely chop the nuts and chocolate.
2   Put the margarine, caster sugar, brown sugar and vanilla essence in a bowl and beat until light and fluffy. Beat in 2 tablespoons of the egg; discard any left over.
3   Put a sieve over the bowl, add the flour and baking powder then sift in. Add the nuts, chocolate and coconut and stir well to bind together.
4   Divide the mixture into 20 or 21 pieces each weighing 50 g (2 oz). Roll into balls, then flatten very slightly to flying saucer shapes and arrange evenly spaced on the prepared baking sheets.
5   Bake for about 10 minutes or until pale golden and the centres feel soft. Leave to cool for 5 minutes then transfer to a wire rack. Serve warm.

Cook's Tips
To toast coconut: spread it flat on a baking tray and pop it under a preheated medium grill. Keep an eye on it all the time. Shake the tray as the coconut browns until it is evenly golden. Do not allow to burn or it will taste bitter.
Brazil nuts have a similar texture to Macadamias – swap them if you prefer.

CHOCOLATE CHUNK COOKIES

Time to make: 25 minutes
Time to bake: about 10 minutes

Makes about 20

1 small egg, size 5
75 g (3 oz) walnut pieces
250 g (9 oz) dark chocolate, 50% cocoa solids
250 g (9 oz) sunflower margarine
50 g (2 oz) caster sugar
100 g (4 oz) soft light brown sugar
2 teaspoons natural vanilla essence
300 g (11 oz) plain flour
1 teaspoon baking powder

These are quite simply the best cookies in the world. Crisp and golden on the outside, soft in the middle with little puddles of melted chocolate. Wonderful. I used to make them for a local health food shop using carob chips and, years later, the shop's customers are still asking for them. These are my can't fail standby for school fêtes and cake sales. Even when cold, the cookies are still slightly soft in the middle.

1   Line two baking sheets with non-stick baking parchment. Set the oven to 170C, 340F, Gas 3. Crack the egg into a mug and whisk lightly with a fork. Roughly chop the walnut pieces and chocolate.

2   Put the margarine, caster sugar, brown sugar and vanilla essence in a bowl and beat until light and fluffy. Beat in 2 tablespoons of the egg; discard any left over.

3   Put a sieve over the bowl, add the flour and baking powder, then sift in. Add the walnuts and chocolate and stir well to bind together.

4   Divide the mixture into 20 or 21 pieces each weighing 50 g (2 oz). Roll into balls, then flatten very slightly to flying saucer shapes and arrange evenly spaced on the prepared baking sheets.

5   Bake for about 10 minutes or until pale golden and the centres feel soft. Leave to cool for 5 minutes then transfer to a wire rack. Serve warm.

Cook's Tip
Measure the egg carefully and don't be tempted to add more than the recipe says or the cookies will spread too much. A cookie, unlike a biscuit, should be crisp on the outside and soft in the middle – even when cold.

PEANUT AND MILK CHOCOLATE COOKIES

Time to make: 25 minutes
Time to bake: about 10 minutes

Makes about 20

| 1 small egg, size 5 |
| 100 g (4 oz) salted peanuts |
| 250 g (9 oz) milk chocolate |
| 250 g (9 oz) sunflower margarine or butter |
| 50 g (2 oz) caster sugar |
| 100 g (4 oz) soft brown sugar |
| 2 teaspoons natural vanilla essence |
| 300 g (11 oz) plain flour |
| 1 level teaspoon baking powder |

Peanuts and chocolate are a very American combination which make great after-school cookies with a glass of milk.

1   Line two baking sheets with non-stick baking parchment. Set the oven to 170C, 340F, Gas 3. Crack the egg into a mug and whisk lightly with a fork. Coarsely chop the nuts and chocolate.
2   Put the margarine or butter, caster sugar, brown sugar and vanilla essence in a bowl and beat until light and fluffy. Beat in 2 tablespoons of the egg; discard any left over.
3   Put a sieve over the bowl, add flour and baking powder, then sift in. Add peanuts and chocolate and stir well to bind together.
4   Divide the mixture into 20 or 21 pieces each weighing 50 g (2 oz). Roll into balls, then flatten slightly to flying saucer shapes and arrange evenly spaced on the prepared baking sheets.
5   Bake for about 10 minutes or until golden and the centres feel soft. Leave to cool for 5 minutes, transfer to a wire rack. Serve warm.

CRISP CHOCOLATE BISCUITS

Time to make: 15 minutes
Time to bake: 10 to 12 minutes

Makes 18

| 100 g (4 oz) dark chocolate, 50% cocoa solids |
| 100 g (4 oz) unsalted butter |
| 150 g (6 oz) soft light brown sugar |
| 150 g (6 oz) self-raising flour |
| 2 teaspoons cocoa powder |
| 1 medium egg, size 3 |

This is a basic recipe that I first learned at college and still cook today. The cookies have a cracked top and a crisp texture.

1   Look out 2 baking sheets and line with non-stick baking parchment. Set the oven to 170C, 340F, Gas 3.
2   Break the chocolate into squares, put in a small non-stick pan with the butter and heat very gently, stirring constantly, until melted but not too hot. Remove from heat and stir until smooth.
3   Put a sieve over a mixing bowl, add the sugar, flour and cocoa powder and sift in. Crack in the egg and whisk with a fork.
4   Pour in the chocolate mixture and stir until well blended. Divide the dough into 18 pieces and roll each piece into a ball.
5   Arrange, well spaced, on the prepared baking sheets and bake for 10 to 12 minutes until the biscuits have spread and the tops have cracked. Cool on a wire rack.

WHITE CHOCOLATE AND ALMOND PASTRIES

Time to make: 20 minutes
Time to bake: 12 to 15 minutes

Makes 9

150 g (6 oz) good quality white chocolate

100 g (4 oz) ground almonds

2 medium eggs, size 3

two 375 g (13 oz) packets bought ready-rolled puff pastry

icing sugar to dust

There is a little French café on the way to the office which does an assortment of freshly baked pastries. Our favourites are the almond ones, dusted with icing sugar, which we buy for each other on birthdays or when we are stressed and in need of a boost. My version, made with white chocolate, is simple but sensational.

1 Look out two baking sheets. Set the oven to 200C, 400F, Gas 6.
2 Break the chocolate into pieces, put in a food processor and process until finely chopped.
3 Add the almonds and one of the eggs and process again to make a thick paste which holds together. Turn onto a work surface and shape into a square. Divide into 9 equal squares.
4 Lightly flour the work surface. Roll each piece of pastry into a 25 cm (10 in) square. Arrange the 9 pieces of almond paste evenly spaced over one piece of pastry. Flatten each piece into a square.
5 Beat the remaining egg and, using a pastry brush, brush in between each almond square.
6 Roll the second sheet of pastry a little more and drape over the bottom sheet. Press well in between the almond squares to seal the pastry. Cut between each almond square to make 9 sealed pastry squares.
7 Using a sharp knife, knock up the cut pastry edges with a horizontal tapping action. This makes sure that the pastry is sealed and will rise evenly. Brush the tops with the egg. Arrange well apart on the baking sheets.
8 Bake for 12 to 15 minutes until well risen and golden brown. Dust lightly with icing sugar. Leave to cool for 5 minutes then serve warm.

Cook's Tip
Choose pastry made with butter for the best flavour.

CHILLI AND BLACK PEPPER COOKIES

Time to prepare: 15 minutes
Time to cook: 10 to 12 minutes

Makes 10

---

1 small egg, size 5

75 g (3 oz) butter, at room temperature

1 teaspoon natural vanilla essence

100 g (4 oz) soft light brown sugar

½ teaspoon ground black pepper

½ teaspoon ground cinnamon

good pinch of ground cloves

½ teaspoon chilli powder

pinch of salt

15 g (½ oz) cocoa powder

75 g (3 oz) self-raising flour

75 g (3 oz) dark chocolate chips

When I was a teenager I used to spend my pocket money on a weekly cookery magazine that built up into seven big encyclopaedias. I used to read it from cover to cover and try out recipes on Saturdays then look forward to the day that the next issue would be delivered to the paper shop. This was developed from one of the recipes I cooked from that part-work over twenty years ago. The biscuits are very chocolatey, crisp and spicy. The chilli is my idea.

1   Look out two baking sheets and grease lightly. Set the oven to 190C, 375F, Gas 5. Crack the egg into a mug and whisk lightly with a fork.
2   Put the butter in a bowl with the vanilla essence, sugar and 2 tablespoons only of the egg and beat well together until the mixture is light and creamy. Discard any left over egg.
3   Put a sieve over the bowl, add the black pepper, cinnamon, cloves, chilli powder, salt, cocoa powder and flour. Sift into the mixture then stir in to make a soft dough. Add the chocolate chips.
4   Divide the mixture into 10 pieces. Shape each piece into a rough mound well apart on the prepared baking sheets and flatten slightly. Bake for 10 to 12 minutes or until flattened and crisp round the edges. Leave to cool for a few minutes on the baking sheets, then transfer to a wire rack to cool completely. Serve with coffee or ice cream.

Cook's Tip
Dunk half of each biscuit in melted dark chocolate and leave to set on a wire rack.

CHOCOLATE DIGESTIVES

Time to prepare: 20 minutes
Time to cook: 20 to 25 minutes

Makes 24

100 g (4 oz) plain flour
200 g (8 oz) wholemeal flour
pinch of salt
75 g (3 oz) butter
50 g (2 oz) white vegetable fat
50 g (2 oz) caster sugar
1 medium egg, size 3
150 g (6 oz) of your favourite chocolate

When we were little, my Mum used to bundle me, my sister and my two brothers in the back of her half-timbered Morris Minor and drive us the 100 miles or so to Granny's in Fraserburgh for the summer holidays. We used to stop halfway in a lay-by and have orange squash and digestives with melted Caramac® on them. It was a highlight of the journey and my Mum tells me that no sooner had we waved Dad goodbye than we would all be asking when we could stop and have the biscuits.

1 Look out two baking sheets and grease lightly. Set the oven to 180C, 350F, Gas 4.
2 Put the plain and wholemeal flours and salt in a food processor. Add the butter and white vegetable fat and process until the mixture looks like fine breadcrumbs. Add the sugar and crack in the egg. Process again to make a firm dough.
3 Lightly flour the work surface and turn the dough onto it. Knead lightly and roll out to an oblong about 5 mm (¼ in) thick. Cut into rounds with a 5 cm (2 in) plain cutter and place on the prepared baking sheets. Stack the trimmings on top of each other and re-roll gently. Cut out more rounds and arrange on the baking sheets.
4 Bake for 20 to 25 minutes or until golden brown at the edges. Transfer to a wire rack to cool.
5 Break the chocolate into pieces and melt in a microwave or in a small pan over a gentle heat. Put a spoonful on each biscuit and gently spread to the edge. Leave to set. Store in an airtight tin.

Everyday cakes

These are the cakes I make if we know that someone is coming to visit, if I need to contribute to a cake stall or have to whizz up something for a child's birthday. The ingredients aren't as expensive, the recipes not as long, and the quantities not as big as for cakes for special occasions. They are informal, family cakes that are worth switching on the oven for.

VERY STICKY PECAN BROWNIES

Time to make: 15 minutes
Time to bake: 25 minutes

Makes 9

175 g (7 oz) **pecans**

100 g (4 oz) **unsalted butter**

150 g (6 oz) **caster sugar**

75 g (3 oz) **soft dark brown sugar**

100 g (4 oz) **dark chocolate, 70% cocoa solids**

1 tablespoon **golden syrup**

2 medium **eggs, size 3**

1 teaspoon **natural vanilla essence**

50 g (2 oz) **plain flour**

½ teaspoon **baking powder**

These come from an American recipe, given to me by a friend in Los Angeles. They are very soft-textured, sweet and chewy, and very chocolatey. I have tried lots of brownie recipes over the last 20 years but this one is definitely the best. They are made by a quick melt-and-mix method and traditionally should be un-iced.

1   Look out a 20 cm (8 in) square, deep cake tin. Grease and flour. Set the oven to 180C, 350F, Gas 4. Coarsely chop the pecans.
2   Put the butter, caster sugar, brown sugar, chocolate and syrup in a small non-stick pan and heat gently, stirring until the mixture is smooth and the chocolate has melted. Remove from the heat and leave to cool.
3   Beat the eggs and vanilla essence together in a mug.
4   Put a sieve over the pan, add the flour and baking powder and sift into the chocolate mixture. Add the pecans and egg mixture and stir well to mix.
5   Pour the mixture into the prepared tin and bake for 25 minutes or until the outside of the brownie is crisp and beginning to shrink from the sides of the tin and the inside is still soft to touch. Leave to cool completely in the tin. Cut into squares to serve.

Cook's Tip
Brownies have a high proportion of sugar which gives them their crisp top. If you are concerned about your health, don't cut the amount of sugar in the recipe – just eat a smaller piece of brownie.

STICKY CHOCOLATE MALT CAKE

Time to make: 25 minutes
Time to bake: 45 minutes

Makes an 18 cm (7 in) square
cake which cuts into 10 slices

150 g (6 oz) dark chocolate, 50% cocoa solids

100 g (4 oz) soft light brown sugar

100 g (4 oz) sunflower margarine or butter

100 g (4 oz) malt extract

150 g (6 oz) plain flour

1 teaspoon bicarbonate of soda

150 ml (5 fl oz) milk

1 medium egg, size 3

This has the texture of a gingerbread but a rich chocolate flavour. It's a great cake to serve plain with a cup of tea.

1 Look out an 18 cm (7 in) square, deep cake tin. Grease and line with greaseproof paper. Set the oven to 150C, 300F, Gas 1.
2 Break the chocolate into pieces and put in a small non-stick pan. Add the sugar, margarine or butter and malt extract and heat gently until melted. Remove from the heat.
3 Put a sieve over a mixing bowl, add the flour and bicarbonate of soda and sift in.
4 Pour the milk into a measuring jug and crack in the egg. Whisk together with a fork until mixed.
5 Pour the melted chocolate mixture onto the flour mixture and stir in. Add the milk and egg mixture and beat everything together to make a smooth, shiny, thick batter.
6 Pour into the prepared tin and shake to level the top. Bake for 45 minutes or until a skewer inserted into the centre of the cake comes out clean and the mixture has begun to shrink from the sides of the tin.
7 Leave to cool in the tin, then turn out onto a wire rack, peel off the lining paper and leave to cool completely.

Cook's Tips
This cake gets stickier and more moist if you keep it for a day or two before eating it.
The grated rind of an orange or the finely grated rind of half a lemon are good in this mixture too. Add them at step 5.

CHOCOLATE MAYONNAISE CAKE

Time to make: 15 minutes
Time to bake: 40 minutes

Makes a 22 cm (8½ in) round
   cake which cuts into 8 to 10
   pieces

275 g (9 oz) self-raising flour

**175 g (7 oz) soft light brown
sugar**

1½ teaspoons baking powder

50 g (2 oz) cocoa powder

**1 teaspoon natural vanilla
essence**

200 g (8 oz) mayonnaise

This is ultra-easy and very quick to whizz together. It uses mayonnaise in place of butter and eggs and makes a very light, moist sponge.

1 Look out a 22 cm (8½ in) round, deep cake tin. Grease and line with greaseproof paper. Set the oven to 160C, 325F, Gas 2.
2 Put a large sieve over a mixing bowl, add the flour, sugar, baking powder and cocoa powder, then sift in.
3 Add the vanilla essence, mayonnaise and 150 ml (5 fl oz) cold water and mix well to make a smooth, creamy mixture.
4 Spoon into the prepared tin and smooth the top, making a slight dip in the centre. Bake for 40 minutes or until the top has risen and the cake has begun to shrink from the side of the tin.
5 Leave to cool in the tin, then turn out onto a wire rack, peel off the lining paper and leave to cool completely.

Cook's Tip
Use a good quality full-fat mayonnaise for the best results.

WHITE CHOCOLATE FROSTING

Time to make: 10 minutes

Makes enough to fill a Victoria
   Sandwich or sandwich 10
   biscuits

**200 g (8 oz) good quality white
chocolate**

100 g (4 oz) unsalted butter

Much, much nicer than old-fashioned buttercream. Use this to sandwich cakes or biscuits together or use it like brandy butter, to melt on to hot puddings.

1 Break the chocolate into pieces and melt in a microwave or over a pan of hot water.
2 Put the butter in a mixing bowl and beat until light and creamy. Beat in the chocolate. The mixture is now ready.

RASPBERRY AND WHITE CHOCOLATE MUFFINS

Time to make: 20 minutes
Time to bake: 35 to 40 minutes

Makes 12

300 g (12 oz) good quality white chocolate

150 g (6 oz) fresh raspberries

250 g (9 oz) plain flour

1 tablespoon baking powder

150 g (6 oz) caster sugar

½ teaspoon salt

100 g (4 oz) butter

100 ml (4 fl oz) milk

150 g (5 oz) thick Greek-style natural yogurt

1 medium egg, size 3

These were voted sensational when my husband took them to work for his colleagues to try. Inside they are tart with raspberries and bursting with puddles of melted white chocolate.

1   Look out a 12 deep-hole bun tin or muffin tray and put one paper muffin case in each hole. Set the oven to 170C, 340F, Gas 3. Chop the chocolate into rough chunks. Pick over the raspberries.
2   Put a sieve over a large mixing bowl, add the flour, baking power, sugar and salt then sift in.
3   Put the butter in a large microwave-proof bowl and melt in the microwave for 20 seconds on Full Power (100%). (Alternatively melt the butter in a small pan on the hob.)
4   Pour the milk into a large measuring jug. Add the butter, yogurt and egg and beat until the mixture is well blended.
5   Pour the milk mixture into the flour mixture and stir to make a smooth, stiffish batter. Lightly stir in the chocolate and raspberries until just mixed.
6   Spoon into the muffin cases, filling each well. Bake for 35 to 40 minutes or until well risen and golden. Leave to cool slightly and serve warm.

Cook's Tip
Unlike a British fairy cake, a muffin has a higher proportion of flour to fat, so they don't keep well. Make and bake them on the day you want to eat them. Freeze any that are not eaten and warm through to serve.

SERIOUSLY CHOCOLATEY MUFFINS

Time to make: 20 minutes
Time to bake: 25 to 30 minutes

Makes 12

225 g (9 oz) plain flour

25 g (1 oz) cocoa powder

1 tablespoon baking powder

150 g (6 oz) soft brown sugar

½ teaspoon salt

100 g (4 oz) butter

100 ml (4 fl oz) milk

150 g (5 oz) thick Greek-style natural yogurt

1 medium egg, size 3

450 g (1 lb) mixed dark, milk and white chocolate chips

For me, these are the ultimate muffins. There is more chocolate than cake mix and they taste of it.

1   Look out a 12 deep-hole bun tin or muffin tray and put one paper muffin case in each hole. Set oven to 170C, 340F, Gas 3.
2   Put a sieve over a large mixing bowl, add the flour, cocoa powder, baking powder, sugar and salt then sift in.
3   Put the butter in a large microwave-proof bowl and melt in the microwave for 20 seconds on Full Power (100%). (Alternatively melt in a small pan on the hob.)
4   Pour the milk into a large measuring jug. Add the butter, yogurt and egg and beat until the mixture is well blended.
5   Pour the milk mixture into the flour mixture and stir to make a smooth, stiffish batter. Lightly stir in all the chocolate drops.
6   Spoon into the muffin cases, filling each well. Bake for 25 to 30 minutes or until well risen and golden. Leave to cool slightly and serve warm.

STICKY CHOCOLATE CUP CAKES

Time to make: 20 minutes
Time to bake: 20 minutes

Makes 12

125 g (5 oz) dark chocolate, 50% cocoa solids

125 g (5 oz) plain flour

3 tablespoons cocoa powder

1 teaspoon baking powder

125 g (5 oz) soft brown sugar

100 ml (4 fl oz) sunflower oil

4 tablespoons hot water

2 medium eggs, size 3

These fall somewhere between a fairy cake and their American cousin, the muffin, both in size and texture. They are moister than either and keep well, getting stickier on days two and three.

1   Look out a 12 deep-hole bun tin or muffin tray and put one paper muffin case in each hole. Set the oven to 170C, 340F, Gas 3. Chop the chocolate into rough chunks.
2   Put a sieve over a large mixing bowl, add the flour, cocoa powder, baking powder and sugar then sift in.
3   Pour the oil into a measuring jug. Add the water and eggs and beat until well blended. Pour into the flour mixture and stir to make a smooth batter. Lightly stir in the chocolate.
4   Spoon into the muffin cases, so each is half to three-quarters full. Bake for 20 minutes or until well risen and firm in the centre.

ROCKY ROAD MUFFINS

Time to make: 20 minutes
Time to bake: 25 to 30 minutes

Makes 15

300 g (10 oz) milk chocolate
150 g (5 oz) walnut pieces
300 g (10 oz) plain flour
1 tablespoon baking powder
150 g (5 oz) soft light brown sugar
½ teaspoon salt
100 g (4 oz) butter
100 ml (4 fl oz) milk
150 ml (5 fl oz) fresh soured cream
1 medium egg, size 3
25 g (1 oz) mini marshmallows

My brother Hamish lives in Canada and it was on a visit to him that I first discovered Rocky Road ice cream – vanilla with marshmallows, chocolate and nuts in it. The same ingredients – but using soured cream instead of ice cream – work brilliantly in a muffin too.

1 Look out two deep-hole bun tins or muffin trays and put a paper muffin case in each hole. Set the oven to 170C, 340F, Gas 3. Chop the chocolate into rough chunks. Break up any large walnut pieces.

2 Put a sieve over a large mixing bowl, add the flour, baking powder, sugar and salt then sift in.

3 Put the butter in a large microwave-proof bowl and melt in the microwave for 20 seconds on Full Power (100%). (Alternatively melt in a small pan on the hob.)

4 Pour the milk into a large measuring jug. Add the butter, soured cream and egg and beat until the mixture is well blended.

5 Pour the milk mixture into the flour mixture and stir to make a smooth, stiffish batter. Lightly stir in the chocolate, walnuts and marshmallows until just mixed.

6 Spoon into the muffin cases, filling each well. Bake for 25 to 30 minutes or until well risen and golden. Leave to cool slightly and serve warm.

Cook's Tip
Mini marshmallows are usually in the baking section at the supermarket. If you can't find them, buy large marshmallows from the sweet section. Cut them into small pieces using a pair of scissors with the blades dipped in flour to stop the marshmallow sticking to them.

APRICOT, ALMOND AND WHITE CHOCOLATE LOAF

Time to make: 25 minutes
Time to bake: about 1 hour

Makes a 900 g (2 lb) loaf which
cuts into 8 slices

200 g (8 oz) good quality white chocolate

100 g (4 oz) ready-to-eat dried apricots

4 medium eggs, size 3

200 g (8 oz) unsalted butter

100 g (4 oz) soft light brown sugar

200 g (8 oz) self-raising flour

200 g (8 oz) good marzipan or almond paste

50 g (2 oz) nibbed almonds

When my Mum came down from Scotland to help me test the typed-up recipes, she declared this one of the best cake recipes ever and flew home with the egg-splattered recipe sheet in her handbag. As a good baker herself, it was no small compliment. The sponge benefits from creamy chunks of chocolate and tart pieces of apricot. It's then layered with marzipan, which melts to a sweet almondy paste. Very moist and more-ish.

1   Look out a 900 g (2 lb) loaf tin. Grease and line with greaseproof paper. Set the oven to 150C, 300F, Gas 1.
2   Coarsely chop the chocolate and apricots. Crack the eggs into a mug and whisk lightly with a fork.
3   Put the butter and sugar in a mixing bowl and beat until light and creamy. Gradually beat in the eggs until light and fluffy.
4   Put a sieve over the bowl, add the flour, sift then fold in with a metal spoon. Fold in the chocolate and apricots.
5   Spoon one-third of the mixture into the prepared tin. Smooth flat.
6   Lightly dust the work surface with cornflour. Divide the marzipan in half. Roll out one piece to a rectangle large enough to cover the cake mixture and put in the tin. Cover with half of the remaining cake mixture.
7   Roll out the second piece of marzipan to a rectangle large enough to cover the cake mixture and put in the tin. Cover with the remaining mixture and press the almonds lightly on top.
8   Bake for 45 minutes then cover with a double sheet of greaseproof paper and bake for a further 20 minutes or until the mixture feels firm in the centre and has begun to shrink from the sides of the tin. Leave to cool in the tin, then turn out onto a wire rack, peel off the lining paper and leave to cool completely. Cut into slices to serve.

Cook's Tip
I have also made this recipe using glacé cherries instead of apricots. Rinse the cherries under warm water to wash off the sugar syrup they are packed in and pat dry with absorbent kitchen paper. Cut into quarters.

MOIST CHOCOLATE CAKE WITH STICKY COCONUT MIDDLE

Time to make: 20 minutes
Time to bake: 40 to 45 minutes

Makes a 20 cm (8 in) round cake
which cuts into 8 pieces

125 g (5 oz) self-raising flour

1 teaspoon baking powder

2 tablespoons cocoa powder

125 g (5 oz) caster sugar

100 ml (4 fl oz) sunflower oil

4 tablespoons hot water

2 medium eggs, size 3

Filling

1 egg white

50 g (2 oz) caster sugar

75 g (3 oz) desiccated coconut

1 tablespoon cornflour

1 teaspoon malt vinegar, fresh
lime or lemon juice

This makes a good eat-with-a-cup-of-tea cake but is also lovely served warm with a thin puréed mango or raspberry salsa.

1   Look out a 20 cm (8 in) round sandwich tin. Grease and line with greaseproof paper. Set the oven to 170C, 340F, Gas 3.
2   Put a sieve over a mixing bowl, add the flour, baking powder, cocoa powder and caster sugar and sift in. Add the oil and water and crack in the eggs.
3   Using an electric whisk, beat for 1 minute or until the mixture is well blended and creamy. If using a wooden spoon, this will take 3 to 4 minutes.
4   Turn half of the mixture into the prepared tin and level.
5   To make the filling: whisk the egg white until stiff, then gradually whisk in the sugar to make a firm, shiny meringue. Fold in the coconut, cornflour and vinegar or lime or lemon juice. Spread this mixture over the cake mixture in the tin, spreading right to the edge. Top with the remaining cake mixture and level the top.
6   Bake for 40 to 45 minutes or until the centre feels springy when you press it with a finger and the cake has begun to shrink from the edge of the tin. Leave to cool for 5 minutes then turn out onto a wire rack, peel off the lining paper and leave to cool completely.

Cook's Tip
For a real Bounty® bar effect, coat the cake in melted chocolate. Put 200 g (8 oz) milk chocolate, 25 g (1 oz) butter and 2 tablespoons milk in a non-stick pan and heat gently until the chocolate has melted. Stir to mix then pour over the cake. Leave to set. Decorate with big shavings of fresh coconut if you like.

MOIST BANANA AND WHITE CHOCOLATE CAKE

Time to make: 20 minutes
Time to bake: 30 minutes

Makes an 18 cm (7 in) square
   cake which cuts into 10 slices

125 g (5 oz) **sunflower**
margarine

125 g (5 oz) **soft light brown**
sugar

250 g (9 oz) **ripe bananas,**
weighed in their skins

½ teaspoon **natural vanilla**
essence

3 medium **eggs, size 3**

100 g (4 oz) **good quality white**
chocolate

50 g (2 oz) **walnut pieces**

100 g (4 oz) **self-raising**
wholemeal flour

100 g (4 oz) **self-raising flour**

This is a great recipe that's ideal for when you have a couple of over-ripe bananas in the fruit bowl which no-one wants to eat. It's a speedy melt, mash and mix recipe that cooks to a sticky cake with generous whole chunks of white chocolate in it. This is another of my great cake sale standbys and one that the children like making with me.

1   Look out an 18 cm (7 in) square, deep cake tin. Grease and line with greaseproof paper. Set the oven to 150C, 300F, Gas 1.
2   Put the margarine and sugar in a small pan and heat gently until the margarine has melted. Stir well and remove from the heat.
3   Peel the bananas (they should weigh about 150 g (6 oz) with the skins off). Put in a large bowl with the vanilla essence and mash with a fork until they are smooth and creamy. Crack the eggs into a mug and beat with a fork. Add to the bananas. Roughly chop the chocolate and add to the banana mixture with the walnuts.
4   Add the flours and melted margarine mixture and stir well to mix.
5   Pour the mixture into the prepared tin. Spread it into the corners and level the top.
6   Bake for 30 minutes until pale golden and springy when pressed in the centre with your finger. Leave to cool in the tin, then turn out onto a wire rack to cool completely.

Cook's Tip
Walnut pieces are cheaper than walnut halves. Buy small quantities, store in an airtight container, and use regularly. Walnuts are high in oil and if kept too long they can become bitter. Check the sell-by date before you buy.

MARBLED DOUBLE CHOCOLATE TRAY BAKE

Time to make: 25 minutes
Time to bake: 30 minutes

Makes 12 to 15 pieces

200 g (8 oz) sunflower margarine

200 g (8 oz) caster sugar

4 medium eggs, size 3

200 g (8 oz) self-raising flour

1 teaspoon instant coffee granules

1 teaspoon hot water

100 g (4 oz) white chocolate chips

2 tablespoons cocoa powder

50 g (2 oz) walnut pieces

This was a very happy accident which has now become a regular feature in our house. I was rushing to make a cake for the school cake sale and in my panic between getting the wee ones to bed and sitting down to watch my favourite television programme I put the cake mixture in too large a tin. Realizing that the cake would come out like a biscuit, I quickly made up a second batch of cake mixture and spread it on top. As I had run out of cocoa, I flavoured the top mixture with coffee and added a packet of white chocolate chips. The result is a moist, two-tone, double-chocolate cake.

1 Look out a 27 x 18 cm (10¾ x 7 in) deep, straight-sided cake tin. Grease and flour. Set the oven to 180C, 350F, Gas 4.
2 Put the margarine and sugar in a mixing bowl and beat together until light and creamy.
3 Crack the eggs into a mug and whisk lightly with a fork. Gradually beat into the mixture until it is light and fluffy.
4 Put a sieve over the bowl, add the flour, sift then fold in with a metal spoon.
5 Put the coffee granules and water in a large mixing bowl and stir to dissolve the coffee. Add half of the cake mixture and the white chocolate chips.
6 Put a sieve over the remaining cake mixture, add the cocoa powder then sift in. Add the walnuts and fold in well to mix.
7 Spoon the cocoa mixture into the prepared tin. Top with the coffee mixture and spread level.
8 Bake for 30 minutes or until the mixture springs back when lightly pressed with the fingers. Leave in the tin until completely cold, then cut into fingers.

RICH CHOCOLATE AND ORANGE LOAF

Time to make: 20 minutes
Time to bake: 1 hour

Makes a 900 g (2 lb) loaf which
cuts into 8 slices

---

1 medium egg, size 3

1 orange

**150 g (6 oz) dark chocolate,
50% cocoa solids**

125 ml (5 fl oz) milk

**50 g (2 oz) butter, at room
temperature**

150 g (6 oz) self-raising flour

½ teaspoon bicarbonate of soda

1 tablespoon cocoa powder

**100 g (4 oz) soft light brown
sugar**

2 teaspoons wine vinegar

This is a lovely mixture that bakes into a moist, even-textured loaf that is good as a family cake with a cup of tea; for lunch boxes or picnics; or warmed up for a pudding – see **Cook's Tip** below. It's an old-fashioned recipe where, if you're short of eggs, you use vinegar to help raise the cake.

1 Look out a 900 g (2 lb) loaf tin. Grease and line with greaseproof paper. Set the oven to 160C, 325F, Gas 2. Crack the egg into a mug and whisk lightly with a fork. Finely grate the rind from the orange.

2 Break the chocolate into squares and put in a non-stick pan. Add the milk and butter and heat gently, stirring, until the chocolate has melted. Stir in the orange rind. Remove from the heat.

3 Put a sieve over a mixing bowl, add the flour, bicarbonate of soda and cocoa powder and sift in. Stir in the sugar.

4 Whisk the melted mixture into the flour mixture. Add the egg and vinegar and whisk well.

5 Pour the mixture into the prepared tin and bake for 1 hour or until a skewer inserted into the centre comes out clean. Leave in the tin to cool, then turn out onto a wire rack, peel off the lining paper and leave to cool completely. Cut into slices to serve.

Cook's Tip
As you only use the rind from the orange in the cake, use the flesh to make a fresh fruit chutney to serve with it. Stand the orange on a plate (to catch the juice) and cut off the pith using a sharp knife. Cut the segments free and chop up small. Stone and finely chop 50 g (2 oz) fresh cherries. Tip the orange, all the juice and the cherries into a small non-stick pan and warm through. Serve with the warmed cake, with a spoonful of crème fraîche or some mascarpone cheese.

ALL-IN-ONE CHOCOLATE SANDWICH CAKE

Time to make: 15 minutes
Time to bake: 35 minutes

Makes a 20 cm (8 in) round cake
   which cuts into 8 pieces

---

125 g (4 oz) self-raising flour

1 teaspoon baking powder

2 tablespoons cocoa powder

125 g (4 oz) caster sugar

125 g (4 oz) sunflower margarine

2 medium eggs, size 3

If you need a quick, reliable recipe to whizz up for a child's birthday, this is it. A classic British Victoria Sandwich given the all-in-one treatment.

1 Look out a 20 cm (8 in) round, sandwich tin. Grease and line with greaseproof paper. Set the oven to 170C, 340F, Gas 3.
2 Put a sieve over a mixing bowl. Add the flour, baking powder, cocoa powder and sugar and sift in. Add the margarine and eggs.
3 Using an electric whisk, beat for 1 minute or until the mixture is well blended and creamy. If using a wooden spoon, this will take 3 to 4 minutes.
4 Turn into the prepared tin and level the top. Bake for 35 minutes or until the centre feels springy when pressed and the cake has begun to shrink from the edge of the tin. Leave to cool for 5 minutes then turn out onto a wire rack, peel off the lining paper and leave to cool completely. Split and fill with Chocolate Buttercream, recipe below, if liked.

Cook's Tip
The eggs and margarine must be at room temperature. If necessary cover the eggs with hot water for 1 to 2 minutes.

CHOCOLATE BUTTERCREAM

Time to make: 10 minutes

Makes enough to fill and cover a
   20 cm (8 in) round cake

**200 g (8 oz) dark chocolate,
50% cocoa solids**

**100 g (4 oz) unsalted butter, at
room temperature**

200 g (8 oz) icing sugar

---

1 Break the chocolate into pieces and melt in a microwave or over a pan of hot water.
2 Put the butter in a mixing bowl. Put a sieve over the mixing bowl, add the icing sugar then sift in. Add the chocolate.
3 Beat everything together until very light and fluffy. Use to fill cakes and meringues.

Special cakes and bakes

Sometimes the only cake you ever make is one for a special pudding, a birthday, an anniversary or for Christmas. You want to be sure it will work, and you want it to be special. I rely on these recipes for all those occasions so I'm sure there's something here to fit the bill for you.

DARK CHOCOLATE ROULADE

Time to make: 30 minutes
Time to bake: 15 to 18 minutes

Serves 6 to 8

175 g (7 oz) dark chocolate,
75% cocoa solids

5 medium eggs, size 3

125 g (5 oz) caster sugar

2 tablespoons hot water

Filling

150 ml (5 fl oz) double cream

200 g (8 oz) good quality
chocolate hazelnut spread

icing sugar to dust

Decoration, optional

150 ml (5 fl oz) double cream

12 toasted hazelnuts

A roulade is a classic cake, made without flour. Rolled up Swiss-roll style with a simple filling it makes a rich and stylish end to a dinner or celebration. There are lots of versions but my favourite uses dense bitter chocolate rather than cocoa powder which gives the sponge a "mousse-y" texture. The cake can be made in advance and the whole thing assembled on the day.

1　Look out a 23 x 33 cm (9 x 13 in) Swiss roll tin. Grease and line with greaseproof paper. Have ready a sheet of greaseproof paper just larger than the tin and sprinkle with caster sugar. Set the oven to 180C, 350F, Gas 4.

2　Break the chocolate into pieces and melt in a microwave or over a pan of hot water.

3　Separate the eggs: put the yolks in a large mixing bowl and the whites in a clean, grease-free bowl.

4　Add the sugar and the water to the egg yolks and whisk with an electric whisk for 5 to 7 minutes or until pale and thick. Stir in the melted chocolate.

5　Whisk the egg whites until they hold soft peaks. Fold into the chocolate mixture. Carefully pour into the prepared tin and gently spread to the edges.

6　Bake for 15 to 18 minutes until risen and springy in the centre and shrunk away from the sides of the tin.

7　Invert the sponge onto the prepared greaseproof paper and carefully peel off the lining paper. Cover with a tea-towel and leave to cool.

8　To make the filling: whip the cream until it just holds its shape. Spread the chocolate hazelnut spread evenly over the cake and top with the cream. Roll up the roulade, from the short end, using the paper to help. Transfer to a serving plate, seam-side down, and dust with icing sugar.

9　If wished, spoon or pipe whipped cream over the top and decorate with hazelnuts.

Cook's Tip
The volume of the roulade will depend on how well you whisk the eggs and sugar, and how gently you fold in the egg white.

RICH CHOCOLATE YOGURT CAKE

Time to make: 20 minutes
Time to bake: 40 minutes

Serves 8 to 10

50 g (2 oz) cocoa powder

125 ml (4 fl oz) hot water

175 g (7 oz) butter, at room temperature

250 g (9 oz) soft light brown sugar

2 tablespoons golden syrup

3 medium eggs, size 3

150 g (5 oz) thick Greek-style natural yogurt

250 g (9 oz) self-raising flour

Icing

200 g (8 oz) dark chocolate, 50% cocoa solids

150 g (5 oz) thick Greek-style natural yogurt

This recipe makes two moist, light cakes which, when sandwiched together with a thick, fudgey icing, make the sort of dense, very chocolatey cake that you might find in a pâtisserie served with a pastry fork and a cup of dark coffee. The icing is simple and makes a thick, very glossy coating that is easy to spread.

1 Look out two 20 cm (8 in) round, deep, loose-bottomed cake tins. Grease and line with greaseproof paper. Set the oven to 160C, 325F, Gas 2.

2 Put the cocoa powder in a large mixing bowl and mix with a little of the water to make a paste. Whisk in the rest of the water and leave to cool.

3 Put the butter, sugar and syrup in a large bowl and beat until light and fluffy. Gradually add the eggs, beating well between each addition to make a light fluffy mixture.

4 Fold in the yogurt and cooled cocoa mixture. Put a sieve over the bowl, add the flour, sift then fold in gently with a metal spoon until the mixture is smooth and thoroughly mixed.

5 Divide the mixture evenly between the prepared tins and level the tops with the back of a spoon.

6 Bake for 40 minutes or until well risen and the cakes have begun to shrink from the side of the tins. Leave to cool in the tins.

7 To make the icing: break the chocolate into pieces and melt in a microwave or over a pan of hot water. Stir in the yogurt.

8 To put the cake together: turn out one cake onto a serving plate and peel off the lining paper. Cover with one third of the icing. Invert the second cake on top and peel off the lining paper. Spread the rest of the icing over the top and side. Leave to set.

Cook's Tip
I sometimes brush each cake with a little marmalade softened with orange juice and sandwich them with fresh orange segments and whipped cream.

SACHERTORTE

Time to make: 40 minutes
Time to bake: 50 minutes

Makes a 23 cm (9 in) round cake
which cuts into 10 pieces

6 medium eggs, size 3

150 g (6 oz) dark chocolate, 50% cocoa solids

125 g (5 oz) unsalted butter

125 g (5 oz) caster sugar

125 g (5 oz) plain flour

Icing

150 g (6 oz) dark chocolate

5 tablespoons strong black coffee

150 g (6 oz) icing sugar

Filling

6 tablespoons good quality apricot preserve/jam

Decoration, optional

50 g (2 oz) milk chocolate

I always think of this as a rather formal, old ladies cake – something you might make if an elderly relative were coming to visit – but it's an ideal dinner party pudding. It's a classic Austrian cake, sandwiched with apricot jam and topped with a shiny chocolate icing.

1 Look out a 23 cm (9 in) round, deep, loose-bottomed cake tin. Grease and line with greaseproof paper. Set the oven to 150C, 300F, Gas 1. Separate the eggs: put the yolks in a mug and the whites in a large, clean, grease-free bowl. Break the chocolate into squares and melt in a microwave or over a pan of hot water.
2 Put the butter and 75 g (3 oz) of the sugar in a mixing bowl and cream until light and fluffy. Beat in the egg yolks and continue whisking until pale. Whisk in the melted chocolate.
3 Put a sieve over the bowl, add the flour, sift then gently fold in with a metal spoon.
4 Whisk the egg whites until they are stiff but not dry. Add the remaining sugar and whisk in. Stir a spoonful or two into the chocolate mixture to slacken the mixture. Fold in the rest with a metal spoon.
5 Pour the mixture into the prepared tin and bake for 50 minutes or until a skewer inserted into the centre of the cake comes out clean. Leave to cool for 10 minutes, then turn out onto a wire rack, peel off the lining paper and leave to cool completely.
6 To make the icing: break the chocolate into squares, put in a small non-stick pan with the coffee and heat gently until melted. Sift the icing sugar into a small mixing bowl and add some of the chocolate. Stir well until the icing sugar has dissolved and the icing is smooth. Gradually stir in the rest of the chocolate to make a smooth, thick icing.
7 To put the cake together: cut the cake in half horizontally and sandwich with half of the jam. Invert onto a serving plate so the base is face up. Brush with the remaining jam. Pour over the icing and spread evenly over the top and side. Leave to set for at least 2 hours.
8 If liked, melt the milk chocolate and pipe a name or message in a flowing script over the top of the cake.

DEEP CHOCOLATE AMERICAN FUDGE CAKE

Time to make: 40 minutes plus
time for icing to cool
Time to bake: 25 minutes

Serves 8

4 medium eggs, size 3

125 g (5 oz) dark chocolate, 70% cocoa solids

1 teaspoon instant coffee granules

1 teaspoon boiling water

175 g (7 oz) soft margarine

175 g (7 oz) soft light brown sugar

200 g (8 oz) self-raising flour

25 g (1 oz) cocoa powder

3 tablespoons milk

Icing

200 g (8 oz) dark chocolate, 70% cocoa solids

170 g (6 oz) can evaporated milk

150 g (6 oz) icing sugar

This cake has a wonderful icing which tastes like melted Milky Way® bars. It can only be achieved with evaporated milk, so even if it's not something you would normally have in the cupboard, do buy some and try it.

1 Look out two 20 cm (8 in) round, non-stick sandwich tins. Grease and flour the tins. Set the oven to 180C, 350F, Gas 4. Separate the eggs into two large bowls.
2 Break the chocolate into pieces and melt in a microwave or over a pan of hot water. Dissolve the coffee granules in the boiling water and add to the chocolate.
3 Put the margarine and sugar in a mixing bowl and cream until light and fluffy. Beat in the egg yolks then the melted chocolate. Beat well until light and fluffy.
4 Put a sieve over the mixing bowl, add the flour and cocoa powder and sift in. Stir in the milk.
5 Whisk the egg whites until they are stiff but not too dry, then fold into the cake mixture using a metal spoon.
6 Divide the mixture between the prepared tins and bake for 25 minutes or until the centres feel springy to the touch and the mixture has begun to shrink from the edge of the tins. Leave to cool for 5 minutes, then loosen the edges with a knife and turn out onto a wire rack.
7 To make the icing: break the chocolate into pieces and melt in a large bowl over a pan of hot water. Whisk in the evaporated milk until well blended.
8 Put a sieve over the bowl, add the icing sugar and sift in. Whisk again until smooth and blended. Leave to cool for 20 minutes. Whisk again to make a thick, smooth, spreadable icing.
9 To put the cake together: split each cake in half and spread with one-fifth of the icing. Put one filled cake on a serving plate, cover with another fifth of the icing and place the second filled cake on top. Pile the remaining icing on top of the cake and swirl evenly over the top and down the side to cover.

ITALIAN CHOCOLATE POLENTA CAKE

Time to make: 30 minutes
Time to bake: 30 minutes

Makes a 20 cm (8 in) round cake
which cuts into 8 to 10 pieces

---

5 medium eggs, size 3

1 tablespoon coffee granules

3 tablespoons boiling water

250 g (9 oz) dark chocolate, 50 % cocoa solids

125 g (5 oz) unsalted butter

150 g (6 oz) caster sugar

125 g (5 oz) instant polenta (pre-cooked maize meal)

icing sugar, to dust

Filling and Topping

200 g (8 oz) mascarpone cheese

1 teaspoon natural vanilla essence

2 tablespoons milk or single cream

1 tablespoon icing sugar

75 g (3 oz) milk chocolate, optional

M y thanks go to my friend Ursula who introduced me to using polenta in sweet dishes and particularly in this cake. Polenta, now widely available, is maize meal and gives the same sort of texture to a cake as ground almonds.

1 Look out a two 20 cm (8 in) round, loose-bottomed cake tins. Grease and line with greaseproof paper. Set the oven to 180C, 350F, Gas 4.

2 Separate the eggs: put the yolks in a medium mixing bowl and the whites in a large, clean, grease-free bowl. Spoon the instant coffee into a mug and add the boiling water. Stir to dissolve.

3 Break the chocolate into pieces, put in a small non-stick pan with the butter and heat gently, stirring, until melted. Remove from the heat.

4 Add the sugar to the egg yolks and whisk with an electric whisk for 5 minutes until the mixture is pale and doubled in volume.

5 Whisk in the melted chocolate mixture and coffee, then fold in the polenta.

6 Whisk the egg whites until they are stiff but not dry. Fold into the chocolate mixture then mix lightly until everything is well blended. Pour into the prepared tins.

7 Bake for 30 minutes or until a skewer inserted into the centre of the cakes comes out clean. Leave to cool in the tins.

8 To make the filling: put the mascarpone, vanilla essence and milk or cream in a bowl. Put a sieve over the bowl, add the icing sugar, sift then beat in until the mixture is soft, smooth and creamy.

9 To put the cake together: peel off the lining paper and put one cake on a serving plate. Top with half of the mascarpone mixture and spread to the edge. Cover with the second cake and remaining filling. Dust with the icing sugar.

10 If liked, melt the chocolate and drizzle off the tip of a teaspoon back and forth over the top of the cake. Cut into thin wedges to serve.

Cook's Tip
Ursula uses 4 tablespoons brandy instead of coffee in her cake.

RICH CHOCOLATE ALMOND CAKE WITH ORANGE & LEMON

Time to make: 40 minutes
Time to bake: 45 to 55 minutes

Makes an 18 cm (7 in) round cake
which cuts into 8 to 10 slices

100 g (4 oz) **good quality white chocolate**

100 g (4 oz) **milk chocolate**

175 g (7 oz) **dark chocolate, 50% cocoa solids**

1 **small orange**

1 **small lemon**

4 **medium eggs, size 3**

100 g (4 oz) **butter, at room temperature**

100 g (4 oz) **caster sugar**

100 g (4 oz) **ground almonds**

50 g (2 oz) **fresh white breadcrumbs**

2 tablespoons **cocoa powder**

Flavoured with lemon and orange and silky with chocolate, this cake has a moist, even texture that cuts well. I make it if friends are coming to stay for a few days because it keeps well, wrapped in foil. It also doubles up as a quick pudding – warm a slice in the microwave and serve with pouring cream or ice cream.

1 Look out an 18 cm (7 in) round, deep, loose-bottomed cake tin. Grease and line with greaseproof paper. Coarsely chop the chocolates. Finely grate the rind from the orange and lemon. Separate the eggs: put the yolks in a mug and the whites in a large, clean, grease-free bowl. Set the oven to 170C, 340F, Gas 3.
2 Melt the dark chocolate in a microwave or over a pan of hot water.
3 Put the butter and sugar in a mixing bowl and cream until light and fluffy. Whisk in the egg yolks and grated orange and lemon rind then the melted chocolate.
4 Stir in the almonds, breadcrumbs and cocoa powder.
5 Whisk the egg whites until stiff but not dry then fold into the mixture. Fold in the remaining chopped chocolate.
6 Pour the mixture into the prepared tin and bake for 45 to 55 minutes until a skewer inserted into the centre of the cake comes out clean. Leave in the tin to cool, then turn out onto a wire rack, peel off the lining paper and leave to cool completely.

BLACK FOREST SURPRISE

Time to make: 45 minutes plus
   standing time
Time to bake: 8 to 10 minutes

Serves 8 to 10

---

100 g (4 oz) plain flour

40 g (1½ oz) cocoa powder

6 medium eggs, size 3

200 g (8 oz) caster sugar

2 tablespoons hot water

Filling

250 g (9 oz) good quality black
cherry jam

300 ml (10 fl oz) double cream

Topping

250 g (9 oz) dark chocolate,
50% cocoa solids

150 ml (5 fl oz) double cream

fresh cherries, optional

I love this cake – it looks great when you cut it. Everyone asks how you do it but once you know the technique, it's easy.

1 Look out a 23 x 33 cm (9 x 13 in) Swiss roll tin and a 20 cm (8 in) round, deep, loose-bottomed cake tin. Grease and line both with greaseproof paper. Lay a tea-towel on a work surface, cover with greaseproof paper and sprinkle with caster sugar. Set the oven to 200C, 400F, Gas 6.
2 Put a sieve over a measuring jug, add the flour and cocoa powder and sift in.
3 Crack the eggs into a large mixing bowl. Add the sugar and whisk with an electric whisk for 10 to 12 minutes until the mixture is the colour and texture of whipped cream and leaves a trail when you pull out the beaters. Whisk in the hot water.
4 Sift the flour mixture over the egg mixture and fold in gently but firmly with a metal spoon. Divide evenly between the prepared tins.
5 Bake for 8 to 10 minutes, until the cakes spring back when pressed and have begun to shrink from the sides of the tins.
6 Turn the cakes onto the prepared greaseproof paper and peel off the lining papers. Cut the round sponge in half horizontally. Spread the jam over the three sponges and leave to cool.
7 Whip the cream until it just holds its shape. Spread over the rectangular cake. Trim edges, then cut lengthways into 6 equal strips.
8 To put the cake together: put one round sponge, jam side up, on a flat serving plate or board. Tightly roll up one long strip, Swiss-roll style, and place in the centre of the round. Add the next strip, winding it round the first and making sure the edges join. Repeat with the remaining strips until the round is covered.
9 Place the other round, jam side down, on top. Cover the cake with the cake tin and leave to stand for 1 hour or until firm.
10 To make the topping: break the chocolate into pieces, put in a small non-stick pan with the cream and heat gently until the chocolate has melted. Beat until smooth, glossy and spreadable.
11 Pile the chocolate cream on top of the cake and spread down the side. Decorate with cherries if you like. For a special occasion, half-dip them in melted chocolate.

TIRAMISU GÂTEAU

Time to make: 30 minutes plus
    chilling time
Time to bake: 12 to 15 minutes

Makes a 20 cm (8 in) round cake,
    which serves 8

**175 g (7 oz) dark chocolate,
75% cocoa solids**

5 medium eggs, size 3

2 tablespoons hot water

**125 g (5 oz) caster sugar plus
extra for dusting**

Filling

4 tablespoons strong coffee

2 tablespoons coffee liqueur

250 g (9 oz) mascarpone cheese

**150 g (5 oz) thick Greek-style
natural yogurt**

Decoration, optional

1 tablespoon cocoa powder

1 tablespoon icing sugar

In Italian, Tiramisu means 'pick me up' and is used to describe a classic mix of creamy mascarpone, soaked sponge fingers and a generous amount of wine or liqueur. I've combined all the typical ingredients to layer up a meringue-light chocolate cake.

1 Look out two 20 cm (8 in) round, deep, loose-bottomed sandwich tins. Grease and line with greaseproof paper. Set the oven to 180C, 350F, Gas 4.

2 Break the chocolate into pieces and melt in a microwave or over a pan of hot water.

3 Separate the eggs: put the yolks in a small bowl and the whites in a large, clean, grease-free bowl.

4 Add the water to the egg yolks and whisk lightly with a fork. Beat into the chocolate to make it smooth and shiny.

5 Whisk the egg whites until they are stiff but not too dry. Whisk in a spoonful of sugar at a time, whisking well between each addition to make a stiff shiny meringue. Whisk the chocolate mixture briefly into the meringue just to blend. Do not over-mix.

6 Pour the mixture into the prepared tins, gently spread to the edge and level the top.

7 Bake for 12 to 15 minutes until risen and springy in the centre and shrunk from the tins at the edge. Cover with a tea-towel and leave to cool. The cakes will stay risen at the edge and shrink level in the centre.

8 To make the filling: put the coffee and liqueur in a mug. Put the mascarpone in a mixing bowl and beat to soften. Whisk in the yogurt.

9 To put the cake together: turn one cake onto a serving plate and remove the lining paper. Spoon over half of the coffee and liqueur mixture. Spread with half of the cheese mixture. Invert the second cake on top and peel off the lining paper. Spoon over the remaining coffee and liqueur mixture and spread with the remaining cheese mixture.

10 If you wish, mix the cocoa powder and icing sugar together and sift over the top to dredge thickly. Chill for at least 2 hours before serving.

CHOCOLATE CELEBRATION CAKE

Time to make: 30 minutes
Time to bake: 1½ hours

Serves 8 to 10

300 ml (10 fl oz) boiling water

75 g (3 oz) cocoa powder

2 medium eggs, size 3

150 g (5 oz) butter

300 g (10 oz) caster sugar

250 g (8 oz) plain flour

1 teaspoon bicarbonate of soda

Filling

350 g (12 oz) dark chocolate, 50% cocoa solids

150 ml (5 fl oz) double cream

1 tablespoon hot water

Decoration, optional

chocolate curls or fresh strawberries

This is the cake I make for family get-togethers – weddings, anniversaries, christenings, birthdays. The cake is very dense, moist and chocolatey and was developed by the team on Family Circle magazine. If the test of a good recipe is how often you use it when results really count, then this one gets a gold star.

1 Measure the boiling water into a 600 ml (1 pt) jug. Add the cocoa powder and whisk to make a smooth paste. Leave to cool.
2 Look out a 15 cm (6 in) round, deep, loose-bottomed cake tin. Grease and line with greaseproof paper. Crack the eggs into a mug and whisk with a fork. Set the oven to 150C, 300F, Gas 1.
3 Put the butter and sugar in a large bowl and beat until pale and creamy. Add the eggs a little at time, beating well between each addition.
4 Put a sieve over the bowl, add the flour and bicarbonate of soda, sift then fold in with the cooled cocoa mixture to make a smooth, thickish batter.
5 Pour into the prepared tin and bake for 1 hour. Cover with a double sheet of greaseproof paper and bake for a further 30 minutes or until a skewer inserted into the centre of the cake comes out clean. Leave to cool in the tin.
6 To make the filling: break the chocolate into pieces and melt in a microwave or over a pan of hot water. Add the cream and stir to make a thick, shiny paste. Add the hot water and beat until glossy.
7 To put the cake together: remove the cake from the tin and peel off the lining paper. Trim off the bumpy and uneven top. Cut the cake into three even layers. Put the bottom layer on a serving plate and spread with a quarter of the filling. Cover with the second cake layer, spread with another quarter of the filling and cover that with the third cake layer. Spread the remaining filling over the top and around the side.
8 Decorate, if you wish, with chocolate curls or strawberries.

Cook's Tip
To sample it at its best, warm each slice in the microwave for 20 seconds or until the sponge is soft and warm and the filling beginning to melt.

DARK CHOCOLATE BREAD

Time to make: 35 minutes
Time to bake: 30 to 35 minutes

Makes 2 x 900 g (2 lb) loaves

15 g (½ oz) fresh yeast or 1 tablespoon dried yeast and 1 teaspoon sugar
450 ml (15 fl oz) hand hot water
750 g (1 lb 8 oz) strong white flour
25 g (1 oz) cocoa powder
1 teaspoon salt
450 g (1 lb) dark chocolate, 50% cocoa solids
1 medium egg, size 3
25 g (1 oz) butter, at room temperature

My colleague Jenny came to work one day with a sandwich made from chocolate bread, mascarpone and strawberries that she had bought in the supermarket. The combination was wonderful – surprisingly not too sweet – and we decided that it was the perfect thing to have with morning coffee if you had skipped breakfast or for afternoon tea if you had missed lunch. The recipe makes two loaves, freezes well and makes a base for the most amazing Bread and Butter Pudding.

1   Look out two 900 g (2 lb) loaf tins and grease well. Crumble the fresh yeast into the water and stir in. (If using dried yeast, sprinkle it onto the water, add the sugar and stir. Leave to stand for 15 minutes until the mixture is frothy.)

2   Put a sieve over a large mixing bowl, add the flour, cocoa powder and salt, then sift in. Make a well in the centre with a wooden spoon, add the yeast mixture and mix well. Use your hands to bind the mixture together into a smooth dough.

3   Lightly flour a work surface and turn the dough onto it. Knead well for 5 to 7 minutes to make a smooth, elastic dough.

4   Lightly oil a 1.8 litre (3 pt) measuring jug. Add the dough, check the measurement on the side of the jug, cover and leave somewhere warm for about 1 hour or until the dough has doubled in size.

5   Turn the dough back onto the work surface and knead again for 1 minute. Knead flat.

6   Chop the chocolate into rough chunks. Crack the egg into a mug and whisk with a fork. Spread or dot the butter over the dough and add the egg. Fold the dough over and knead again. When the mixture is smooth again, knead in the chocolate.

7   Cut the dough in half and shape each into an oblong to fit in the prepared tins, arranging it so that the seam is on the bottom. Stand the tins on a baking sheet, cover and leave to rise for 15 minutes.

8   Set the oven to 210C, 425F, Gas 7. Bake the loaves for 30 to 35 minutes or until well risen and the loaves sound hollow when you turn them out of the tin and tap them on the bottom. Leave to cool on a wire rack.

INDEX